A Little Dose of Grace of Jesus

Volume 3

CeCe

Dedication

To everyone who reads the books that my niece shares with the readers. These include stories that describe her life through these dedicated books. I would like to say that it's an honor, a pleasure, and a privilege to share with you my thoughts about my niece, and also to offer her my congratulations on her books that she puts forth to give God the Praise and Glory on His healing within her life and the others that provide her the testimonies of their healing and blessings as well.

She has always been a very kind-hearted and thoughtful person. I believe she was born with an entrepreneurial spirit. From early adulthood, she pursued her calling unto God. She has spent mostly all of her life supplying uniforms, which put her in one of the best places that she could have been. Doing this job allowed her to meet people from all areas of the government. The task also allowed her to get to know some of the different spirits of God in working. They may have good jobs, but life's task still hits everyone the same way. Her stories share the things that people shared with her, as the story about her uncle and me in this book. My niece is a born again Christian and truly spends her time sharing the word of God freely within her church and work, and everywhere she goes. She has spent time sharing and bring the same love of God to our church too, which is The Word of God

Fellowship and Christian Center Church at 1610 Main Street, Conyers Georgia, where her Uncle John T. Smith is the Pastor and I the First Lady Catherine Smith.

She always brings people to worship with us when she visits us. She has had many challenges within her life, this is so true, yet God has kept her through it all, and He will do the same thing for you as well if you trust and believe in the spirit of God and let him take control within your life as well. He is the one and only true living God, and He is always the same, yesterday, today, tomorrow, and forevermore if you trust and believe in Him.

To God, be the Glory for He has done great works within her life and is still doing greater works, as she grows more within the spirit of God in her life.

Auntie, First Lady Catherine Smith

Word of God fellowship and Christian Center

Acknowledgment

This book goes to the parents that God had given me. They both have passed on to be with the Lord, in the flesh, but living in my spirit daily. I walk under the anointing of leadership from them for sure. God placed these parents within my life for seeking knowledge and as His Blessings. They taught me to serve Him within everything I do. The continuing Blessing of the healing and God within other people's lives as well. We walk in the unity of God to give back today's blessings by doing our duties. We promote Jesus' healing and blessing openly unto the world for faith, healing blessing, and relief of the daily tasks within our lives today. It's truly the same God!

He did it in the days of the Bible, and He's doing it today if we only believe and trust Him. God never leaves us alone, as He's always there for us in our daily tasks present in our lives; no matter how hard or bad they are, He's there for us. We are not alone, but others are dealing with the same problems that we face today. We are not talking to them, and they are not talking to us, as well.

That's where *A Little Dose of Jesus* is born from; helping one another through the eyes of Christ daily—leading each other with the promises and faith for one another by believing in Christ. Helping our brothers and sisters stay strong within the words of Christ for us should be the True goal. Helping tear down the walls of disbelief within someone else's life for the healing of Christ. He did it for me, and I'm not special! He'll do it for anyone else according to their will and trust in God. I'm a steadfast believer in the healing and power of God, for every one's life with Him. I'm sharing stories of my walk of faith and blessings that I have enjoyed. The same must have crossed someone else's path in Christ as well; if we only give it to Him!

About The Author

CeCe is a servant of God. A true servant! Not only in my conversations, but living in my everyday walk of life. For God has had favor all over my life. He has shown me who He is within my life. The guidance of Christ for healing and blessing of Him. To restore everything that the devil stole from me within my life. I don't look like all the things that took place within my life. My life has had so many ups and downs, but God has always remained constant. The healing and blessing of God have made my life bearable, allowing me to have the faith to overcome whatever was placed in my way. It includes the grace to keep faith in God regardless of the pain that I was feeling.

There are scars on my natural body as a reminder of how far I have come and the healing from the test that I just passed in Christ. For example, when I attend the church to fellowship among the saints of God, I'm always waving my left hand, although I'm right-handed. It is just to let God know how much I thank Him for healing it from being paralyzed. For yet today, I can use my left arm and leg; being able to walk again, without a walker or cane; being able to wave unto Him in praise for doing what doctors said that I'll never be able to do again, without those aids. For standing on the words of God in trust and belief that He'll do it for me. Holding Him to His word for the asking. It didn't happen in a day or a week. It took some time, and honestly, I don't remember how long, but it happened, just like He said it would as my final outcome. Also, that's more than enough for one's healing. Today I move as I did twenty years ago. I still have some shortcomings to keep me praying for belief in Him. Just give your worries to the Lord and leave them there. Don't go back and pick them up because you feel He's not moving fast enough. Just wait on God's relief for your favor in your life of Him. He won't run out on you, so don't run out on Him, but standstill on the voice of God for your own healing and blessing. If He did it for me, and I'm no better than you, He's waiting on you as well. Come, let's go and have a Holy Ghost time in the Lord. Giving true praise where praise is due.

Millions of people give praise to the wrong ones all the time. Why? Because they look like the one that they are looking at in a mirror, and they are genuinely their God, for sure. They drop their names as if they are the healer, the savior, and the one covering them. I find something wrong with that, for sure! The living and true God, we can't even breathe without Him, and that's where they are lost.

The titles that a man gives himself mean nothing without Christ in his life for real. The material things that they have accomplished before people stand for nothing when Christ isn't in it. The list of vices goes on. No God, No peace, and it just doesn't make sense to go to hell through the Church! But then we must also realize the reason Jesus had shut the church down. Today, the churches aren't much better either. They are working as large, network marketing places. They do more click groups, as well. There is no unity among people. They spend more time on things that have nothing to do with the salvation of God's people than anything else. These people are still lost for the lack of knowledge of Christ, yet technology has the whole world within their hands. Food for thought, if the people of God were carrying themselves in the same Godly manner with which they treasure their phones, what a wonderful world this would be! Instead, they sell themselves as the world does, instead of being in the world and not of the world, but Christ.

Contents

Page Left Blank Intentionally

Introduction

Well, every day is a journey in this world that we live and call it our life. Every day, living is a challenge for sure. In fact, daily walking in my life alone is indeed material for producing books. That's not just me, but everyone in the world as well. These books are about daily tasks with people that cross my path and the things that they share with me as well. The walk of life is lonely, and most of the time, we don't talk to anybody while we are going through. But we're never alone; others are wearing the same shoes, just not talking and communicating to you. When we share the battles that life throws our way, we are winners in Christ. And when we throw in the towel, then we are losers, it's just that simple!

Winners never quit, and losers never win. So, let's join hands and take our lives back with a storm and ensure the devil gets no victory with us in this world. This is not a girl thang, nor is it a male thang, but a Holy Ghost Fire thang in Christ, and that's enough for everyone who wants to win. The choice is always ours because God gives us free will within everything in our life. We have to choose Him to move forward, it's that simple; come ride these books of everyday living with me for faith, hope, and new dreams of the glory of God's will for our life. Share the dreams and visions that God has put into you with others who look just like you. It's that simple, and the blessing will always stand before all of us in the unity of God for our lives daily; for every day we live, it's a new little dose of Jesus keeping us. We have favor in God, in spite of ourselves. As you read, do a lot of thinking. Think about the times you were in the same shoes as me and others, and how you handled it. Which way was the road you took, and why? What was your outcome? How long did you battle the devil that was attacking you? How many times or days you went to God for an outlet before you were released from the curses or witchcraft that was standing in front of you?

Understand the *"its"* that came your way. Remember, you are not alone; millions of people are attacked the same way, but fail to talk to you. I suggest you come, take my hand, and go along for this ride on the heaven highway with Christ as the Healer within our life. He released blessings with your name on it. He'll restore your life, just for the asking and heal your body without a bill for the healing in Him because no one can repair our life like God, and it's all for the asking of Him to take control within your life. I'm a living testimony of the healing, blessing, and restoring one's life through divine command. And so can you be as well!

Chapter 1 - Daily Plans, My Trike?

The blessing of the Lord is truly a daily task within our lives. For the blessing and grace are stored and applied to our lives as we walk with Him. We should never take the grace and mercy for granted, but that's just the way we live as well! All the blessings of the Lord are for granted until we get the heartbreaking news or something happens that we can't handle; then the shift kicks in, our eyes open wider, and our thoughts become different as well. It's the little things that truly mean so much in our lives, as if God owes it to us, like the air we breathe when we open our eyes in the morning.

Someone had planned for a trip this week and saved money to do it with, in the bank and have a fine house and a fast car, and the list goes on and on, but they didn't do anything they had planned because they died last night! You got up with the problem of no money in your bank account and didn't feel like going to work today, and that's all before 8:00 this morning. The grace of God got you up, and you didn't even stop to thank him? When you get paid on Friday, you can't wait to get yourself a drink because of the fact I heard you say: I can't wait to get drunk this weekend? I stop and wonder, who wanted to work all week and when they get paid, get there drink on? Millions of people can't wait to party and plan to get as drunk as they can, and you know the rest. Well, grace and mercy keeps them in this state of mind with hope for their lives and the Church never cross their minds, unless it's a funeral. Even at that time, they never think of the fact that this could have been them? The Grace of God is nothing to play with, but many people do it. They think God owes them something, and there are as many in the church as out of the church.

They come but never really find God's love for His people first, and they don't even love themselves either. The put the act of Christ on the big show; that's what I call it, but never live anything close to Christ's message within their lives. We must always keep Christ first, as the head of our lives and trust the grace and mercy that He and He alone has over our lives, and we won't be missing what God truly has in store for our lives with Him.

And the Lord shall utter His voice before His army: for His camp is very great: for He is strong that executeth His word: for the day of the Lord is great and very terrible: and who can abide it?

Therefore also now, saith the Lord, turn ye even to me with all your heart, and fasting, and with weeping, and with mourning:

And rend your heart, and not your garments, and turn unto the Lord your God: for He is gracious and merciful, slow to anger and of great kindness, and repenteth Him from evil.

Who knoweth if he will return and repent, and leave a blessing behind him; even a meat offering and a drink offering unto the Lord your God?

Blow the trumpet in Zion, sanctify a fast, call a sole man assembly:

-Joel 2 11-15

For the Lord is our guide in this road, called life. The shortcomings lay within us, and not in Christ. The still voice of God leads and guides us daily, but only if we are listening to him? For if Christ is for us, then nothing in the world can destroy us. For this morning, I was exiting my garage, and the third car garage door opened up for no reason at all. I saw my motorcycle boots, and something said put those boots on today. Well, I said, *they are too heavy, and I'm not putting on those boots* and shut the garage door.

Well, for no smart reason at all, I was on my trike. I didn't leave from my usual front, but made a U-turn there and for no sane reason, I let up the clutch too fast and took my foot off the running board, and put it on the ground and cut off part of my foot, as if I needed it to stop when the bike jumped, and I required it to hold the bike up. Now on two wheels, you do need to hold it up but not on three wheels, and then I saw me bleeding out. Part of my five

5

finger shoe was cut off and my foot as well. I drove all the way home like that. Blood was everywhere, hitting car windows and everything, and as I drove, I was praying to God saying: Lord there are three beds that I could be going to right now: first, the hospital because I do need a doctor; two, I could end up in the morgue, if I bleed out; and then three, my bed that you, God has already supplied me with? Well, I went all the way home with blood splattered all over the bike and clots so thick that I could barely shift the gears, but I made it! Well, my God-daughter lives in Detroit and had been trying to call me. I don't ride with my phone on me, but in the luggage carrier on the bike. So when I got home, I answered the phone and she was saying why you haven't been answering your phone? Then I explained to her what happened and she told me to send her the picture of what was going on with me.

One of my postal customers and her children were coming over to see me as well. Her six-year-old daughter said, come on, Ms. CeCe, and let me clean you up when meanwhile she (customer) and her eighteen years old were afraid of the blood and condition of my foot. So we cleaned it up, and I went to bed. Well, my goddaughter called and said she didn't get the pictures and I said that I had sent them? Oh, but I sent them to a guy that works with my oldest son. He then took them into the office to show my son what had happened. No, me being who I am, I wasn't going to tell my children. They live far from me, and I felt no need to tell them, but as soon as he told my son, the chain began to move.

He called me upset then called my younger son, and he came too, to take me to the doctor. I felt that I prayed and was fine, but he felt differently about it. He's a minister and still doubts my faith in God. He told me that there is a thin line between faith and foolishness, and right now, I'm being foolish for sure. We went to a doctor, and all they did was give me some cream to put on it that probably wasn't much better than the cream I already had at home. My son wanted me to get a tetanus shot because he said I have diabetes, but they didn't even want to do that! That's what they said, but I believe that my faith has healed me for sure. Their actions were out of love for their mother, for sure.

Chapter 2 - Learning Love

Last week, I cried myself to sleep on Sunday, saying, Lord, no one loves nor care about me! Well, sometimes it doesn't matter how good you think you are with the people that call themselves the children of God, they still mistreat you for nothing, nothing at all. And this was one of those times in my life when I felt as if people were treating me so badly for no reason at all? From the pulpit to the pews, it seemed just like that, and that spirit was moving in everyone. I said praise the Lord to get relief. Well, when I got home after service, it was about 2:00 in the evening, and it was Mother's Day.

Sure, I wasn't looking for any of my children nor grandchildren. I like to keep it real. So I'm dressed early for bed today and ready to enjoy some well-earned good night's sleep, as I wouldn't have to share the afternoon with anyone else. I have one special prayer daily: Lord, can I get up and go to work in the morning? Well, to some people, they look at me as if I'm crazy, but to others that truly know me and the life tasks that I've overcome, they understand. After being blind, paralyzed, and the list goes on then, they know why I just want to work. I work six days a week and give God back his Sunday and Bible study during the week. If you have a Friday night service, just call me, and I'll be there. I can run from church to church all day on Sunday, and whoever calls me or sends me an invite, I'm always there! The churchgoing is truly over us, and it's Kingdom time for sure! The world is going through so many changes, to wake up the true children of God and push the church back in the closet, where they belong. No teaching anything nor living anything unto God! Just pulling numbers in chairs and never learning nor living the bible that's at hand. We must learn and live it for ourselves if we plan on going to heaven for real. Then, when I woke up on Monday morning, the Lord said that for the weeping endured last night, I'm going to show you, My love, today. Well, when I first wake up in the morning, I begin to pray before my feet hit the floor. This morning I started praying and prayed myself back to sleep, and when I woke up again, it was 8:14 the second time.

Then I said to myself, Lord, I got to get out of here before I'm late for work, and then He told me to slow down because He's going to show me love today. Well! I got up and got dressed and went downstairs to have a bowl of cereal and leave for work. When I got the garage door open, I realized that my son's friend that I've been letting stay with me wasn't gone to work yet either, so I called out to him to ask why he was still there, and he replied that God told him to move slowly this morning, just as He had told me. When he got downstairs, he said, why don't you ride your bike today? I replied that God told me to get in that Q56 today. And that is what I am driving today. He came down to move his work truck to let me out the driveway, and we started talking for a few minutes, and then I left.

When I arrived at my subdivision entrance, I realized that traffic was all backed up as I took the right turn, out of my subdivision, and it was at a haul today. Well, when I got to the first street as traffic moved forward, I saw a tractor-trailer, then a brand new SUV, and it was bent in, into a U. Well, the first thing that came to my mind was: if I had been on that bike, that could have been me dead on that bike. Then they were in an SUV, and it was a U, the S and V was gone by the shape it was bent in. Then as I proceeded to work, every road that I was traveling on, I saw car accidents that looked as if people lost their lives in them.

As I reached the shopping center where I work, I was on the phone with the head mother of the church that I attend, telling her what I've seen this morning, and I couldn't figure out what was happening this morning at Burger King? Well, as I passed Burger King and began parking my truck, one of my postal customers was already sitting there, waiting on me. He stated CeCe, I've been here since 8:00 waiting on you.

He stated he got off at 7:00 and thought that I open at 9:00 instead of 10:00, but he waited to use his postal card before going home to go to bed. Well, he said that he saw everyone running out the Burger King, and then police were flying over there like crazy. Later, we learned that a guy got shot and killed in that Burger

King. Well, here's the love of God. That morning my youngest son had passed by and saw all the police and stuff that was going on and wanted to know where his mother is this morning.

Then, later his wife passed by and called him to say she saw all the police and stuff but didn't see my car and they started calling and looking for me. Then the phone in the store and my cell phone started ringing crazily from people that were church members, customers and the list goes on to see if I was alright. God showed me love in a situation where someone else had lost their life. Well, the mercy and grace of God keep falling over me at all times in my life. While still feeling unloved and uncared for all that week, God kept showing me His love and grace.

I received calls from people that I haven't seen in years, and they told me that even though they don't see me, they are always praying for me and that they love me. Well, I've had some people tell me that they love me, but I couldn't tell. They never pick up the phone and call me just to say hello, and neither do they ever take time to answer a text from me either, and the list goes on; when I try to reach out to them, they are always too busy for me.

I've found that people make time for what's important to them, and I guess that I'm not. And they love me, so they say but if that's love, let's say I wouldn't want to get on their bad side and we are doing all of this in the name of the Lord, but I can't find Jesus anywhere in this action at all. I pray for the mercy of God that keeps with me at all times within my life. For you are a merciful God and will always get the praise from me!

Chapter 3 - The Trike Ending

People have been telling me that I'm too old to ride a bike and other foolishness statements. I thank God that I don't listen to people. They open up their mouths with nothing good to say at all, and they wonder why they can't lead me and why I'm not following them? They speak death unto my life instead of life, and they sit and want something bad to happen to me for what reason? I guess I'll never understand that, but they do, and they do it so freely and still call themselves Christians, as they speak death unto you?

All I can say is WOW! Then I stop and look at them, and they don't live half as well as me, but are always trying to lead me, to where? Is what I want to know? You must always take time to watch as well as pray, and I'm watching even when I'm not praying; the devil is always mad at me because I don't give him the space to grow in my life.

But anyway, they told me that I would need a surgeon to put my foot back together and when they called me days later, I told them I had one, Jesus and He's all that I need, and He heals and doesn't send me a bill! Well, they said it would be months before I can wear shoes again, but in three days, I was back in my toe shoes, and on Sunday, I plan to wear my heels to the church, because that's the kind of God that I serve. He is always better to us than we are to ourselves, but the next time I get on that bike, not only will I have my boots on, and my safety gear is worn, but I will also use other provisions. Yesterday, I made myself a safety vest with CeCe at the top, a cross in the center, and rider on the bottom; but most of all, the lettering is in red, for the blood of Jesus covers me at all times within my life. For as we walk, He walks with us, and there are truly times that He carries us, and this is one of the times in my life that God is carrying me.

As I look back over the past two weeks and look at the mercy, blessing, and grace of God in all the things that I've seen and heard, well, who wouldn't serve a God like this one? For serving God is my greatest passion in my life, not just because of the healing but because it takes nothing from me to give him time in my life. Sometimes, I'm at work with not one customer in the store all day, and that doesn't become a day of putting up stock or doing anything else for the business, but a day of praise for God's anointing all day long. It's always something for me to do at work, but whether I want to do something is very different.

Mostly when I do have customers, I talk their heads off. Whether it's about their uniforms or just everyday life and if I know they serve God, then it's on and popping, and they know when they come into the store, the one thing you don't do is come, when you don't have time to waste with me. But for the most part, they all usually show me love, and sometimes I can take that for granted because I'm standing there too closely to receive what God has already given unto me. Then when I feel as if no one cares, He reminds me quickly who I am, and then that's enough for me. For the grace and mercy of God should never be taken for granted, but given the credit that it deserves within our lives as we walk daily in him. For God's grace should never be looked at, as if He owes us something? We don't ever look at the glass half full but always half empty? If He fills it up, we are still not satisfied? The more He gives unto us, the more we want from Him for free without the commitment of truly serving Him for who He is within our lives.

We will never be able to pay God for the worthiness that He showed to us first, nor are we going to be able to serve Him enough as well. The more we give, the more is required of us as children of God for His mercy and grace upon our lives. When we think that's the task of daily life is about over, well think again, because as long as we live, more is required of us, as servants unto the Lord in our walk with Him. We can't beat God's giving and goodness in our life, and we never break even with Him.

The more we try, the more we must put forth an effort to remain in his perfect will for our lives with Him. The small things that we go through are for gaining strength in Him, and we must always show our worthiness to Him as we walk. He won't let us down, and we must keep pressing forward in Him if we plan on making it successfully. Things will come and go, and we must keep faith to show our strength in God. For a while, I thought my accident was something until I saw a young man walking around the parking lot where I work and carry a dumbbell that wrapped around his body. Well, me and the lady who works with me on Saturdays. As he approached the storefront where we work, he asked me why I was limping. My reply was that I was in a motorcycle accident. He then replied, that's how he lost his leg and had four plates in his collar and back from a motorcycle accident himself. He told me this, too, will pass by the grace of God. He then replied that even though all that had happened to him losing his leg and everything, he still rides motorcycles. My children, mainly my sons, want me to stop riding, but people have car accidents and still drive cars? And when he told me about all that he had gone through in the past two years, he believed that God spared his life, and he also bought himself a new bike.

Riding has a whole new feeling and made a huge difference in his life now, but he still rides! Well, I plan on being back on my bike within weeks. They say it will take a year or more for my feet to heal from the inside, but I say: they don't know my Daddy! He heals in spite of what man might say, and He restores without a bill, and I've already got my boots out and stretching them because of my scars on my feet, let's say the shoes don't fit! But nevertheless, I will be riding again real soon as I believe God has control over all things within my life, and there is nothing the devil can do about it, but watch me as I move in the power of God! For all things, we must give thanks to Him within our lives.

No matter what the test may be, we must still give God the praise. Things don't always look as we make them appear within our lives. Sometimes, we put too much into worldly things. This man's story makes mine look like nothing? The test that he passed was life-threatening for sure, and he kept his faith in God, moving forward in his life with the proof is in his walk.

Chapter 4 - Where Is the Movement of God?

Neither is there any creature that is not manifest in his sight: but all things are naked and opened unto the eyes of him with whom we have to do. Seeing then that we have a high priest that is passed into heavens, Jesus, the Son of God, let us hold fast our profession.

For we have not a high priest which cannot be touched with the feeling of our infirmities; but was in all points tempted like as we are, yet without sin. 16 Let us, therefore, come boldly unto the throne of grace, that we may obtain mercy, and find grace to help in time of need.

-Hebrews 4:13-16

Well, grace and mercy come from the throne of God. He's the only one who can give grace and mercy unto us. Man, and when I say man, I mean mankind, both male and female will come in and out of our lives for whatever purpose, but God never leaves us at any point in our lives, even though we sometimes feel as if He has, but that's never true. Sometimes, we think we are at our lowest that we can go in our lives, yet God is always standing there waiting for us to do well. Some choices that we make may not be good for us, but we make them anyway, and then we look for someone to blame besides ourselves? As we go down, so does our faith and trust in God as well, but He is not the problem, for we are our worst enemy when we are not listening to Him. We put so much trust in ministry that it's unreal; instead of putting all our faith and trust in God, and when the ministry fails us, should we leave the church? Now, what sense does that make? The Bible tells us that man will lie, steal, and kill us. So when they get busy in our lives making mischief, we blame God and keep running behind people, we truly put our trust and faith in other than Him. I know this only too well.

I've trusted people so many times that it is unbelievable, and then the thanks that I get after believing in them is always a mess. They stand up before us wearing fine clothes and spreading the gospel as if they, for one life according to it, and then pretend as if they have no fault within themselves as well. For the most part, I can say today with an open heart and mind that I've met some of the biggest liars in the Church.

They were the leaders, or should I say the pastors of the church and nothing in the pulpit was right. It hurts to even walk into a church when I know they aren't living right! As a matter of fact, I can't walk in at all into such places. They can't preach to me, and they don't speak to me either, because those devils know who they are fooling and who just ain't buying their lies! Then every time some of them say anything to me, money is always involved in the conversation. I feel as if that's the only reason that they keep asking me to come back? If they ain't talking about money to me, then they ain't talking to me, so what gives? I don't like people who are always asking me for money. I find myself worth more than what I put in an offering or have given to the church. What happens to believe in the love of God in everything and experiencing the grace and mercy of God in the Church? If they aren't doing multi-level marketing of some kind and a show to get big bucks from you, then they don't waste any time trying to know your name and suffering.

When I was growing up, well, just let's say this, we lived in the church. We were there sometimes three or four times a week. They had prayer service and several other services. They didn't time the movement of God because, honestly, you can't, but today, everything is on a time list and doesn't go one minute over as if it's professional service! There's no testimony service of what God did for you today nor this week.

Sometimes I want just to shout out what God did for me, but mostly I do that at my work with my customers or in my home by myself, just giving God praise for all that He's done for me every day. My praise to God isn't on a timesheet but at all times in my life. I can't praise Him enough. When you can only praise at times, you are sure not living the right way and do not know God as your true savior, protector, and giver. The praises should always be falling off your tongue day and night. You can't thank Him enough, and you can't give up on God because He doesn't give up on you. I wake up four or five times a night, and I pray every time my eyes open from sleep. If I get up and go to the bathroom, I dance to the bathroom and back. If you know what I've been through, then you would understand. Sometimes we take God's grace for granted. But the truth is God made our body so perfect, and to lose any part of it and not be able to do something as simple as putting on a shoe, you would understand what I'm talking about.

Today, I went to buy shoes although I have plenty of them in my closet, I can't get them on my feet? So I know God is going to heal my foot, and not because I said so, but because He said so. This is only a test, and I'm wearing the pain of my foot and leg well. No, I can't put on shoes, and I'm still swollen. In fact, my whole body has put on thirteen pounds since my accident, but I always give credit to God because I could have lost this leg or foot as the gentleman had whom I had met, but again, God's grace and mercy had me covered.

Then at some point in our lives, we must take responsibility for our actions and not blame God nor anyone else. When we reach this point in our lives, we then begin to grow where we stop putting our shortcomings on others and look hard at the image we see in the mirror. That mirror never ever lies to us if we take responsibility for ourselves instead of blaming whoever we can. I find myself taking deeper looks at myself instead of others. It's not that I can't see them, but we are not supposed to judge others, but we do it all the time. We should look at the fault in us instead of others as it is the Godly way of doing things. Do you have people that you talk to, although you don't ever want to hear their voice? Well, I do! They never have anything good coming out of their mouth, ever! They find fault in everyone else but never visit the reality in the mirror? They can't seem to ever have peace with anything, including the church, and they think I'm crazy? Well, here's some soup for you! Sip it slowly, and don't miss one drop because you need this to grow.

For one thing, have you never visited that mirror? Then, are you happy with what you see? Then, what can you do to fix yourself and your life problems, and stop acting like you are watching out for others! This is a very true statement to grow on; it takes six months to mind your business and six months to leave everyone else's alone, and the year is now gone. Then, let's bring the New Year in singing this same old sad song! Let's see how much happier this world would be if you do work for yourself and let others do the same, including me! We all have our own minds, and we never will be on the same page because that's the way God made things. Even when people get married, they face many problems, trying to make someone be like them instead of letting them be who they are, and then we can all have a good day. Most people fall in what they call to love with someone, never realizing who they are, not at all. Then if they get to the point of marriage, they start trying to make them who they want them to be. They never accept them as they are, although letting them be who they are, and working around them are the best choices. This makes life better for all the involved parties at this point in their lives. This is so important for having a healthy relationship in your life. It's a whole lot of give and take, to make a house a home. And the central element that we need is love between those house walls. It is essential to take part in relationships equally, although I don't know anything about it.

I have heard of this concept, but it wasn't present in my parent's marriage, and I've never had it in my relationships either. Well, I never had it because I didn't put much into a marriage, but always looked for great rewards out of it. But I can now say that is what most people do, and they don't get hip to it as I do. No, things weren't ever easy, and that was a fact, but grace kept me going all these years that I went through absorbing so much heartbreak and lifelong pains in relationships. Then the role that most people play was never any good for me. I'm sure my ex-partners will make good husbands with the training that they got off living with me? They learn to respect a woman with me, man up as a caring father, and the list goes on. At this point in my life, I've been married as many times as the days of the week, seven I should know who, what, when, and why not of relationships by now! There was this guy who asked me to marry him, and I'm still trying to figure out why? Let's see, he talked to everyone but me and kept telling me so much stupid stuff. Yet, I know God for myself and also that the devil is a liar and a thief if you allow him to misuse you in his web of lies. Then he's in your ear talking what you think you want to hear? Then the most prominent part is that God said so, but if you don't know the actions of God, then you will get caught up in the web of lies that are placed before you. As I say, I've been there and done that already, so I can only fall for a new trick that you devil haven't already used on me?

The faces have changed, but the game is still the same, and you already have got me once. Shame on you, but if I allow you to get me again, shame on me, so at this point, we are going to leave it on you! God enables us to go through these tests just for providing an understanding that the strength is in Him and as a lesson for you to grow on. If we didn't go through them, we wouldn't have anything to pray for, although we truly need God daily in our lives.

Grace is like a circle, and it keeps on going around if you are serving God. It doesn't quit on you as you stand by Him. The best part is that you can fall off by the wayside of Christ, but He never falls out on you! I used to feel as if I've seen it all, but if you keep living, you keep learning. However, I have found no new game but only new players playing the same one. For Some people, you think that it's not working for you today, and it didn't work for you in the past, but you are truly amazing because you're still trying it instead of seeing your shortcomings in life.

God knows that I have strived in my lifetime, and I don't have issues with myself nor anyone else because I've grown in this area of my life. Get a grip on yourself and realize that it's not about you only. You should never try to make it seem as if you're that important, but only people that look just like you. But where are they following you? That's what I thought, nowhere! Only what we do for Christ will last, and everything else will sink in the quicksand. It's so sad because most people don't see this shortcoming in them, and you can't tell it to them either; just pray that God will open up their eyes before it is too late.

We are living in a dying world today, and everything written in the Word is already all over the world? Times are indeed getting harder, and the days are getting shorter. I think that people are not looking into what's really going on in the world today. They are missing it. The rumors of wars and all the horrible things that are arising today are real, and the sad part about it is that we don't have anyone watching over our wellbeing, not in our government or the church, and nowhere else. They aren't looking out for anything other than their pocketbooks, and they are always trying to see how much bigger they can get? The rumors of wars are real and not far from us today. I don't watch the news, but when I'm on my computer at work, I see all the bad stuff going on in the world. And at this point, I begin to pray for others who seem far away yet are closer than you might think. God is still watching over all of us, however, although we aren't taking care of ourselves. We take grace for granted in so many ways and don't really realize how close to our front door it is.

Chapter 5 - Time out for Games

Among whom also we all had our conversation in times past in the lusts of our flesh, fulfilling the desires of the flesh and of the mind; and were by nature the children of wrath, even as others.

But God, who is rich in mercy, for his great love wherewith he loved us,

Even when we were dead in sins, hath quickened us together with Christ, (by grace ye are saved;) And hath raised us up together and made us sit together in heavenly places with Christ Jesus.

That in the ages to come he might shew the exceeding riches of his grace in his kindness toward us through Christ Jesus.

For by grace are ye saved through faith; and that not of yourselves: it is the gift of God:

Not of works, lest any man should boast.

-Ephesians 2: 3-9

We are all guilty of our sinful ways within our lives. There are no big or small sins, but all are the same unto God's eyes. Still, we spend so much time judging people in their walk of life. The

God that we serve makes room for all of us at every place in our lives. If we are not where we need to be, He's right there to give a helping hand. If we are slipping from where we are, He's still right there. After we get ourselves together and start running, He's always there for us after the storm has passed over in our life.

Some people never get it together. I find that people would instead run a con game all day, then work for the things they need in their life. If you are at a gas station trying to buy gas, they come up to you with the story that their baby needs some pampers, although they are smoking a cigarette? They cost the same as pampers, and I wonder what need was more important for such people since it's all a game for them; it doesn't matter.

I had a person who worked for the post office tell me that people love to give support to others on the street. So his full-time job was panhandling. He put on dirty clothes for this job. When he came one day to shop for his postal uniforms, I had to ask why you are so dirty, because I saw him get out his new Mercedes car, and he looked like he had been working in the yard. Well, he told me that he makes about two hundred to three hundred dollars a day, and he has never cashed his postal check as panhandling pays all his bills every month for the past twenty years.

People love to give to the poor, and he looks for them when panhandling. He has a sign that says that he's hungry and his dog is too. When he told me where he panhandles in the morning, I was delivering some uniforms to a school near that area and saw him myself doing all he could to take money from innocent people who like to give. He's just one person, but millions do it every day and in different types of ways; some do it on a pulpit in the name of the Lord while Jesus has nothing to do with it. It's all about them and not anything due to Him.

But surely, they will answer for their actions, and when I run across people that don't believe in the power of God, it's mostly because of people like the one that I have described who lead them wrong and instill fear of being fooled. This results in many people losing their faith in God. The love of God is always present for our asking within our life if we trust Christ and not the fake people who come to lead us unto their wickedness in them and not Him.

Grace has kept me pushing forward in spite of everything else that comes my way in my life. The mercy of God keeps me strong at my weakest hour, and the blessing of the Lord keeps following me as I walk with Him in my life. Mercy and Grace will always lead you to a higher level in Christ. We should remember that Christ is still at the head of everything in our life, only if we are listening to Him. Then the choices and roads of our life become easier to travel despite all the troubles.

Perhaps some people get so caught up in the game, they no longer know right from wrong in their lives. They put on such a big show that they begin to believe it themselves. Meanwhile, they are missing the blessing of God, and so are you running behind them, wasting your time. The truth is always the truth, and you never have to fix it up. All you have to do is lay it out plain, and everyone around you will know who you are and what you believe in Christ. The words of God are always something to grow on. You walk in the anointing of God so that you won't ever have to keep looking over your shoulder and losing sleep over the false front you put on for people. The lies and games get harder as the days go by, and there's nothing you can do about it. But with Christ, all the blessings and grace fall unto your foot as you walk with Him in your life. I spent the days at work all this week and did not really do much of anything at all, but worked on this book.

Well, one might say that wasn't good for business, and no money came from it as it won't pay my bills, but God has a greater plan in all this. He knows that I still can't move as well as I would have been before I hurt my foot. Well, it's not just the foot, but my entire leg and moving around isn't easy. When I focused my mind on staying with Jesus and His blessing to come forth to help me, I made out my bills as I always do but did not mail them as of yet because my bank account does not have money. The bills are now sitting on the file cabinet. Well, this is nothing new for me, but the blessing of the Lord is always refreshing to me. I know that God will release some funds for me, and from where they will come forth, I'm not sure.

But I'm sure of one thing, it will happen because God said it will and that's enough for me. Well, one day I was so broke, and all I could think about was that at five o'clock, the phone company will turn off my phone today. Then, a woman that I didn't even know came into my store, handed me a card, and told me not to open it until she left. Well, of course, I'm hard-headed; as she was walking to her car, I opened it up, and there were five new hundred dollar bills in the envelope. Of course, I chased her to tell her that she couldn't give me that money. Well, she replied that God told her to give it to me, and I can't stop her blessing. Well, I did use it for the purpose that God gave it to me for, and again thanked that God's blessing and grace fell down on me. You just can't beat how God will provide no matter how hard we try.

Grace and mercy come down in so many ways and show the favor of God. Well, a few minutes ago, I called my youngest son about this day, and the lady and the money that she gave to me. He remembered it as well and then reminded me of something else. When I had come out of a coma, I used to do many crazy things. One was that I would make the statement that I'm back! Well, I wasn't back, but I kept saying that, and today my son told me, Ma, you're better, but you are still not back and reminded me of so many things that happened in this period of my life. When one is trying to get their life back on what they might call the track, well, let's say this, the one truly successful is the one who knows who you were before and what stands before them today. He stated that I'd come so far, and he thinks I still have some way to go. Well, I feel as if the grace of God has kept me, and I too can say I'm not what I used to be, but I'm not looking for that old me either. God has kept me in His care so much over these past years, and the grace and mercy of Him have taken control of my life; I'm not mad at Jesus, not one bit, but thank Him for who I am today. Once you move out the old and take in the new, don't look back but keep pushing forward unto God who strengthens you.

People in your past will always remember who you were, and they can't even see who you are today. Well, you know that's enough for us, as we walk that long lonely road on the path of God and always remember, I'll go, even if I have to go by myself. Oh, it hurts sometimes and brings tears to my eyes when I think where I am and remember where I was, but nevertheless, don't take yourself through it because the greater reward is always in front of you.

Sometimes we find ourselves lusting after our past, and that's when the devil gets the victory in our life if we allow him to. They call it depression. Not being able to let go and let God take over can tear your life apart. Sometimes you must give up family and friends, and change jobs or even your church to move forward. God knows the bigger picture and always has a better plan for our life if we are listening to Him. Some of the stuff we think we need in our lives and just can't live without, well, we really don't need that in our life. And it wasn't right for us or had any value within our life, but we couldn't see it. Nevertheless, it wasn't within our favor at no point in life. Sometimes it's sad because we really can't see the big picture nor know how to make the changes that we need for a healthy life. Sometimes, I get big kicks out of the silly stuff. I let people talk to me as if I'm a fool, but they are only fooling themselves.

Then I play the drum roll while I realize the game; the whole hook and bait lined up for me. You don't like to show your entire hand but walk with their plan of nowhere in your life; while praying that they run into Jesus for real. God wants more for us than we want for ourselves, and often better for us as well, and we miss it with such games. We are our worst enemy and don't even realize it. Keeping your head up helps but is not always the best answer. Keeping Christ first in every part of your life is the ideal answer!

Chapter 6 - Getting Your Praise On

God got us! God is the fundamental key to everything that comes our way. God's way is supreme in the church, schools, home, and everywhere that one might go. As we learn to look at the glass half full instead of half empty, we can win what we call everyday life. As my mind moves forward, leaving the things of the past. Oh, how good God has been to me! I just can't praise Him enough. God has saved me so many times, and I could never praise Him enough for what He has done in my life.

Sometimes, I listen to the same songs all day long, looking for relief from God in song and praise of others. It's very important what one feeds their spirit. These songs come from the heart of people that are singing unto the Lord. The words say it all, and when someone sings, and you can feel it in your heart and soul, they are saying something important. Have you ever had people stand before you preaching, but when the service was over, you couldn't tell anyone what the service was about? I know people that sit in church and say: that was a beautiful service, and when I asked what it was about, they couldn't say anything! Well, he might have been preaching, but you weren't listening and learning anything from it.

Then you hum the song, not truly knowing the words; I know it didn't touch your heart because you didn't feel the pain behind the words. Probably they were caught up in the music? Then they miss the glory of God and what He has brought for them. They truly don't know Him, and He doesn't know them either in return. It's a shame to sit in the church and make all those fake noises, but never truly learn about the grace and mercy of God.

Some people that I know run from coast to coast chasing ministers and making sure that they get front row seats but again still don't know God but only show the behavior that they have practiced and learned. Your walk is personal with God, and people will come and go. If you're watching, you can see them come up and go down in the walk that they are truly practicing in their lives. But only what you truly do for Christ will last.

There is no falling down in Him; believe that! For there are only two ways to everything in the world; the good, the bad, the right, and the wrong. But your worthiness is only in Christ, who always speaks for you. When they stand up before you speaking what they might call the truth, well, you better beware of them. Remember, a liar and a thief can't tarry in the eyesight of God, that's to let you know He's not in it. Don't let their good looks and well-spoken manner fool you, because practice makes them look perfect in your eyes, but God knows better.

I've been bitten by that bug myself. They come with their fancy games, and they know how to use you to get what they might want from you. However, time is the best teller in everything, including my bank situations. I always say that banks never lie in my favor when some utility bills collector states that they have not been paid. This is everyday life because the games that people play in our lives are genuinely crazy. The funny part is that there is no end to their behavior. Meanwhile, they mess up one's life so much that it's truly crazy to think of. They feel that they are so smooth in their actions that you might miss it, but God doesn't. He's always ahead of the game that we call daily living. He has complete control over our lives.

He guides us if we listen to Him, and His grace remains over us if we stand still hearing His voice, and then the mercy comes and cleans everything around us. For the difference God makes in our lives is greater than all the turns that one might make by themselves. Sometimes, God grants us things that do not look good for us, as well. The grace of God should never be taken for granted. Sometimes, God wants more for us than we want for ourselves. Sometimes, He allows us to have things that aren't good for us but showers us with His glory back when we realize that we didn't need those things as they weren't right for us anyway.

I've found times like today when the preacher was preaching that he made me look at myself. He stated how lucky women were to be able to wear makeup and wigs and other stuff to make themselves beautiful. Well, as I listened I began to look around the room, the men dye their hair and beard and what a man might do today to hide their age, well, let's just say this: they do as much as women today, but I thank God that I outgrew all the silly stuff. I'm not in hiding from anybody. I do not use any hair dye, and my face never gets foundation because God has given me a foundation, and I'm pleased with the foundation that He gave me.

However, one of the lady ministers today went on to hug me and messed up my white usher dress. She put her foundation all over my dress, and I'll be lucky if it comes out after washing. Personally, what a man sees is what he's getting with me. I've gotten too old for all the fake nails, eyelashes, and other stuff. Some of it I've never had like false eyelashes, and I used to dye my hair before the grandchildren came, but they changed all my dye and nails.

I now bypass all the wigs and the fake things that are available in the market. When I see some people, I wonder if they stop by the mirror and take a look at themselves. Then they can find that they are pleased with what they are doing and not happy with how God made them. Most men don't like all that stuff, and similarly, most women don't like all that stuff that men are doing as well. I once told a man who asked me to take off my hat and put some curls in my hair or even a wig on and some nails? Well, if one lost their hair due to illness or something of that sort, that's different but to take and make a mess out of one's self, that's crazy. Don't get me wrong; I do wear eye shadow sometimes. I've been told that I look better without it. That might be true since I'm no different from anyone else. My ex-husbands have always disliked makeup on me. They say: you don't need that mess on your face. To be honest, I went out of my way to make them mad about it because I felt it was my choice, and they should've let me be if that's what I wanted to do.

I wore makeup since I was about twelve years old. Now, my mother didn't wear makeup or approve either, but you should know the rest as girls do; I would sneak and put it on. Well, if she was looking for a street woman and not a virtuous woman of God because that's who I am today and I don't let any devils tempt me. It is something I haven't ever done and never will because that's not who I am.

Last night I went to a Christian birthday party. They had a minister who did comedy, and he didn't move me one bit, but I was praying for him. He made jokes and said he was brought up Pentecostal, but today he is pen-Baptist. Well, God didn't split any fence, and neither should we, but again, people do all kind of stuff and say: it was in the name of the Lord. Well, I am Pentecostal, and I've made no change because the Church is in me. I dance all the time but when they were in a church line dancing, well if I could, I wouldn't take part in that. Then there are so many things churchgoers do in the church today; it's amazing that they do everything in the name of the Lord. Someone is going to answer for all of this stuff that they do in an ungodly manner. The dinner was excellent, but all I could think was the minister's display of comedy was nothing but full of devil's work. We should never get so comfortable in the house of God for no reason at all, and I'm sure that's why they didn't have it in their church. A matter of fact is that I could bet on it if I gambled. Sometimes we think just because we changed the address that it's okay, but the truth is God's still there, and He sees you, and you're not fooling Him.

Like I know it's hard to look some people in the eye knowing the life that they live outside of the church walls. Their family sure does the acts of unity, but what they do, let's say oh my God! They are funny mainly because I don't care what they do, yet the people around you talk. They talk about you, whether you are good or bad, but what they speak and say about you is entirely on you. I know people talk about me, but like I heard a preacher say today, sometimes they are judging you and don't even know your name. This is true because I've attended a church, and from the pulpit, they talked about me, and until today, they still don't know my name.

They made a comment on my dress attire and car but didn't know that they might have degrees, and I don't have them, just have a good daddy, Jesus Christ, and that's enough for me. He's the keeper and restorer of my life, and the only thing that I live for daily and all that I ask is: Lord, can I go to work in the morning? I want to work 23 more years doing uniforms as I build my ministry for Him, and the holy word says He will give me my heart's desire if I give it to Him. Yesterday, I was told that I was a fool wanting to work that long. Well, they don't know the mission that God got me on, nor the masterful plan that God has placed within these hands, but I do. And they will come forth not because I said so, but because God said so, and that's enough for me.

When people spend all their lives in church but never have any growth, it is because they aren't truly committed to Christ and never find anything wrong with their life at all. They sleep around and sit up in church, judging others when their own kitchen isn't clean. But they aren't hiding from God or other people because what's done in the dark always shows up in the light, albeit quicker than one might think. How can one love God and hate their brothers they see every day? Easy, they don't love God in the first place, and they don't even love themselves. They become faultless within their own eyes and their own minds and remain stuck right there! They have no growth in them because nobody can tell them anything for their own good. As I sat and listened to the preacher, my mind went to wander through all kinds of stuff. For example, I think that my eyes look quite nice without false eyelashes. Sometimes, I'm in my car and can see another woman in a car driving across from me, hers are so long and appear to look like they are falling off. Well, if God had made them that long, we would be complaining about them; but since He made them of the right length to protect our eyes, we go buy some foolish product that's falling down on our eyes.

The list goes on as I can see so much ungodliness in the room across from me. I wouldn't trade places with any of those women that I look at any time in my life. All I can do is thank God for the mother that I had, and I still messed up in some areas, that's called everyday living, and we all have shortcomings along the way. God grants us time as well to get our life together before it's too late, and I felt as if I was running out of time. Time waits on nobody, and the world is getting more wicked every day.

Some people see it for what it is, and so many others can't see past their nose. They have no relationship with God, and therefore, they know of no peace in their lives. Neither is there any hope for them, as they are truly lost souls out there, and they aren't looking for remedial help. They laugh at the church until something happens in their lives, and then that's the first place that they run to. God's mercy is always there but should never be taken for

41

granted, but we do even as the saints of God, we all fall short of the glory of God.

He's always standing still and waiting on us. We have people in powerful places, and they say that they are looking out for us, but we better be looking out for ourselves. God gives us wisdom in all things if we are listening to Him and attain the guidance that comes from Him. I know that I don't listen as well as I should, and when things go wrong, I go back to my Godly thought, as I wish that I hadn't doubted God's word at all in the first place.

He stands still and waits on us to run back to Him, although He has already warned us first. The pain is always too much for me to bear because being a churchgoer all my life and then becoming a Christian in the latter part of my life, I can see the fault in me and wish I had listened back then, but I'm like most people. I waited until I reached rock bottom to try to put it all back together again.

Chapter 7 - Breaking Life Chains

Breaking it all down, I always heard old people say: you're going to keep hitting your head until you bust it wide open. Well, that was putting it lightly. Some people just see me and ask: what have you done now? They are always looking forward to some crazy thing to be going on with me, every time they see me. And usually, I've got something going wrong in my life. Some come to look at me at work with nothing other than they were just checking on me, knowing all of the things that I've been through. But God knows that I'm just sitting still and waiting on the grace of God for completion in my life.

He's going to bring everything that I haven't had before. He is the Man, above men. I say to be truthful unto God first, and then, you can get everything that a woman could want in a man. Now, today, I had a man tell me that I was going to be a lonely old woman and stuck by myself. Well, the devil is a liar for sure! Now, I don't want him, nor am I looking for anyone else. The Bible says when a man finds a wife, he finds a good thing and has favor with the Lord. I'm not looking, nor am I allowing the devil to mislead me anymore with all the false prophets out there who bring no good news for me.

I've been there and seen their works for sure, and I've learned that I must sit still and wait for what God has for me! I know that he will be first true unto God and faithful, loving, caring, and so much more, but most of all, he will have Jesus at the head of our marriage, and everything else will fall in place. I'll know who he is as well because the spirit of God will lead me and guide me correctly for attaining completion in my life. Every woman wants a Mr. Right, but they run into so many wrongs before they ever meet him; that's if at all they ever meet their Mr. Right. I'm a pro at making this mistake.

Sometimes we want it not to be perfect; we try to sell the dream to ourselves; that's typical men and women for you. We see it as they are not hiding it; we makeup whatever we can to justify it, but never truly buying it, and lastly, but most importantly, we haven't sold it to ourselves but still praying for relief of a relationship that was dumb from the start. God showed it to us, and we didn't want to believe it could happen to us.

And we sit there and try to make it be a success, but we knew that wasn't the right answer. Well, time waits for none, and we are only fooling ourselves, so in the end, we are back where we started from, still lonely. We wasted time being unhappy when we could have been happy if nothing else by ourselves. Well, when God sends the special someone, you'll know it without measuring. It's nothing more significant than that mate that God prepared for you.

You will never doubt that mate, and you will know, and they will know as well that you are a perfect match. You should know that two people will always have some kind of problems because they can never agree on everything, but you'll have more great days than bad days, and you'll never go to bed upset with each other. When you guys have Jesus at the head of your plate, everything will always be great! Grace and mercy have everything to do with it. As I'm writing this, the truth is there are more lonely days than joyful days, but with Christ, I'm still quite all right.

People must first be in a relationship with their selves and find out who they are, and get peace with themselves before trying to love someone else. I'm over fifty and growing older each day, and now as I look back over my life, the person I truly hurt the most was me! I did myself no good in all of the marriages, and I missed my children growing up as well and tried to buy my way out because I was too busy working or trying to get rest, just to go back to work.

There were times I had two or three jobs, and grace again kept me standing in spite of myself. I couldn't be much of a wife less a mother, but I did try. If money could buy it for my children, then they got it, but I didn't do any hugging and kissing, but they were always dressed to impress, and that is what I called love! Today, God has let me learn the true meaning of love and whenever I get married again, all that I didn't have before, is all in me for the man that God will send me as a husband, for he will be as worthy of me as I am of him. Grace will keep us together till death do us part, and we will grow older and wiser as the years go past; but mostly, all the things in our past will be so far behind us, and the love and grace of God will be in front of us. As we walk, the life changes will fall deep in the back of our minds, never to come up within our marriage because God will cover the walk with all of His blessings as we walk in unity together. For what God puts together is always everlasting in Him. The stuff we put together becomes messy, with relationships having horrible endings a lot of times if we don't get out of them fast. Grace holds us and keeps us in these hard times within our lives if we are there with Christ on our side. Grace smooths the tears away, calms the heart, and restores our minds from all the foolish decisions that one might have made for themselves.

Giving it to Jesus is the only way to grow and move forward in our lives. Things will come and go, and we will always have problems within our lives as long as we live, but how we handle them is something else and who we trust to handle them with us as well. God did give us five senses, and we probably don't use them well most of the time. What we see is not always what we get, but what the devil puts before us, we take it for good when there is no good in it at all for our wellbeing. Then it smells so sweet unto our nose, and the smell is of sin unknowingly unto our nose but comes across as a summer rose. The touch is so softly felt like nothing we have touched before, and we just think about the words that flow from their lips and how touching they are unto our ears and heart. And the list goes on, I'm sure you get it. But without God, it's all unholy unto him, and the wage of sin is death. Death doesn't always mean dying physically but dying in the stuff that we have allowed us to get caught up in. But once we turn it over to God, the light goes off, and we start seeing things differently within our lives. The walk that used to be so smooth and the lust within one's eyes that used to look so good, well let's say we now have a change within our lives and the mercy of God just saved us in the nick of time before we were lost eternally without Christ on our side. The roses of God never fade away, and the lust for Him never dies.

And the purpose of Him always stands up strong within your life, and you will find yourself always having your mind stay on Him, and the blessing of Him always making you push forward in Him alone, and then you find times you wonder how did I truly make it without Christ as the head of my life. When people were putting me down and using me for all they could get out of me in the name of a friend or family member in their own needs and not yours, you still try to help them in spite of their selfishness. When I felt as if I need someone to be there for me, I found myself all alone, and the only one that I could call on was Jesus as my savior.

He made time to stop by my house and show me love and take time to hear my cry and let me spill all my problems on His shoulders, and that was all I needed in my life at my time of need.

God showed up and heard my cry, and He slowly but surely filled the gaps within my life and restored the lost hope and the broken heart with pure blood flowing through it with love, in spite of all the broken promises and lovely lies and the list goes on. God grants your heart with His fullness. He replaces the bad in your life with small doses of His mercy. As I walked, the load got lighter, and the sun shined brighter. See, I believe that God and only God is a healer at all times in our lives. Life will knock you down, and it seems there is no one who might care around, it appears that you might have more rainy days than sunshine, and the clouds are just following you around.

Then, when you stop moving so fast and give it to the Master of masters of problems and the only one with a correct answer, then that shift change comes and the sun starts peeking out just a little bit at a time; and when you rise in the morning, you find yourself just thanking God for waking you up in the morning with a clear mind and ready for the tasks ahead. Meanwhile, knowing that you just put Him at the head of your day. I find myself doing this before my feet hit the floor, for God comes first in my life and the days are much brighter with Him at the head of my every day of walking with Him, for things do still happen, but I can handle them differently with Christ on my side. There are many troubles that have our names on them, but with Christ, they seem just to come and go without any effect on me because of who I put at the top of my plate each day. Then and only then, I feel like I breathe the fresh anointing of God all day long, and no devil can stop me in spite of anything that they might try to do to upset my daily walk. When we change our way of thinking, then things change in our way of living as well. For the Bible says: so a man thinks, so is he. Soft and sweet but so true because

I find myself that people think that I can do everything, but honestly, I'm not that smart. They give me credit that I shouldn't get, and at other times I cut myself short. We all have this battle within oneself. You truly know your shortcomings and strong points, and nobody has to tell you that, but it's nice when people see you for who you genuinely are. I've had somebody tell me that I try to dress to impress the preacher which is so far from the truth.

The clothes in my closet have been there for thirty years, and clothes don't make a person, not at all. They can dress nice, but their attitude is so ugly that it doesn't matter what they wear; they still look ugly. Let's say: that suit or dress looks nice but who's wearing it? Clothes don't make a person, but the love of Christ does. It's not what you put on the plate and what you did for the church, but what's in the heart of the person that counts, and it's not because the church gave so much credit but only what you do for Christ will last. If it's the fashion show before men, well, you got that, but for God, the true walk of your life is what counts, and you can't fool Him? The word says: what does it profit a man to gain the whole world and lose his soul? Well, they can't buy their way into heaven, but to the eye of a man, it might look good. I personally find the words of God to be my guide for a happier life, and I don't spend my time trying to get praise from man. God sent three to keep us at all times. The Father and the Son and the Holy Spirit. The Father is to love on us in spite of everything going on in our life; the Son to guide us in the flesh as He stood where we now are; the Holy Spirit is the keeper of our souls until we meet again. We can't survive without these three in our lives, no matter how hard one might try, and we always find ourselves falling back on each one at different times within our lives as we live.

I once heard a songwriter say these words in a song: I can't live without him! Well, that was enough said: we can't live without Him and that's enough said. When you reach that time in your life, and you truly find God for yourself, you'll understand what I'm talking about. It took me almost my entire life to reach this point. Being in church all my life had nothing to do with it, and that's how I know whether people are real or playing games.

I've been there and seen that all before, and I used to be one just like them. I went to church on Sunday and cussed you out in the parking lot if you caught me wrong in those days. Today, they try me but have no success at all because I got Jesus, and I really don't need anyone else. Oh sure, I smile and laugh and talk to them, but I know who they indeed are, and the fool is them, not me. I'm the same every day. I don't change because anything else is fake, and that's not me.

Once a man asked me to take off my hat and add some weave or a wig and said that you can put on some nails too. Well, he wasn't talking to me because I'm not fake but a child of God, and what you see is what you get. And if we spent more time being who God made us instead of trying to change, well, let's just say we would be happier. What one might call it doing to make them look good is a mess, and because they make it in a bigger size does not mean you should buy or wear it?

When I was one pound from three hundred, well, let's say there were times that I had to stop by the mirror and check myself. I do thank God that I didn't think everything in the stores' plus size was for me. Then I had some family that kept on top of all things when it came to my dressing. If it didn't look good, believe me, they said so. God covered me in so many ways that I just can't tell it all. But every day, the grace of God keeps me in many small favors, and I don't take it for granted when we look at my past and stop and give God praise because sometimes we are so blessed and don't even know it.

If I never get another new car, I thank God for the cars that he has already given me. If I never have another house, I thank God for the home that he has already given me. If I never get another new dress or pair of shoes, I thank God for the dress and shoes in my closet, because what I take for granted some people have never had the pleasure of owning and I misuse my blessing sometimes because I can be selfish. I told a friend today when she told me to give away some of my clothes. I replied that I bought them for myself, and I am going to keep them for myself; it wasn't an option in my life. Well, she doesn't know me as well as most or for as long. I've given away truckloads of clothes and a bus full of them and sent them to Africa, and the list goes on, but the road of helping people I took was taken for a fool and misused by people. We have all been there at some point in our life, but we should learn from it. People have said and done all kinds of stuff to me, but the grace of God has allowed me to move forward.

Today I was asked to be the president of an usher board. Well, I'm a servant of God, and it's not wearing the uniform but selling it. I'm a true servant of God in so many other ways, but it's not behind the walls of the church. I'm not looking for praise from men, but get it from the glory of God within my life as I walk. Many people just look at me in the church, speechless. They don't know if they can talk to me, and they look even crazier at me.

Sometimes, it's the dress, and then it's the dance, but mostly because they truly don't know my Heavenly Father as I do, so they don't understand! Then grace falls differently on each one of us according to our relationship with God. They can't even see the difference, but there is one. The commitment in Christ is a standard in your life, and you don't play with that, not all the churchgoers do it all the time. They clap their hands, but it's to the music, not the Lord. They scream and fall out, but it's the attention that they want but not praising unto God because everything you do for Christ and when He moves, it's in order.

He's an orderly God. From the beginning, everything was done in order, and when you know the Lord, you know the difference. I know we are not supposed to judge people, and I'm really not, but calling it as I see it because I know them by their names, and they are not true children of God. They can fool some people around them, but true children that do things unto God are not moved by only a big show. We come in a few numbers, and we are not fooled by the tricks of the devil, nor are we moved by them either.

I find myself lying to myself about shopping. My rack in my closet fell down, and all my shoes and clothes on that rack were all over the floor. Well, I said on Thursday, I'm not buying anything else, I lied, and today I stopped on my way to church and bought a sweater and shoes that I don't need. But I sold it to myself that I work so hard and should be kind to myself because no one else will. Well, this is not true, not at all! God's good to me all the time, and I'm still not happy with myself. I truly don't need anything, nor should I be buying anything, and after I do, I end up seeing something else that I might want because I don't need anything. God allows us to do things sometimes that aren't good for us in shopping and in a relationship and in all the roads that we take in our lives. We must take control of our own shortcomings in our life. He gives us guidance, and we have to do the rest ourselves.

God's so patient with us in spite of what we do to ourselves and how we repay Him. We don't! We just keep piling up our mess until we cannot run from ourselves anymore, and then we run straight to Him to dump all our trash out on Him, and if we aren't careful, we blame Him as well. Being who He is, He still showers us with His loving grace and mercy and keeps on blessing us regardless of what we have done wrong. Well, I had an ex-husband ask me for money, and I started speaking the word of God to him that he knows so well, he hangs up the phone. He doesn't want to hear what I have to say but still want my money.

Really? Well, I told a friend of mine that I know him so well that when he gets over my no, he'll answer the phone for me and he did today. I told him no on Friday, and he replied today on Sunday. Sometimes it takes weeks but anyway, that story that I'm going to pay you back, well it's played out. I know that he's never going to pay me back because he makes no effort to pay me back what he has already stolen from me. Anyway, you still want more? Well, that's stupid of you and not stupid of me because the God I serve teaches me not to allow people to misuse me regardless of who they are, or what they call themselves as well. They wear all kinds of titles on their names, but what are they truly living up to? These lights blink for themselves, and everyone isn't wrong, and you're right. I can remember before I married him, people asked me, do you know what you're getting into! Well, I don't judge people by what people say, but I do about what they do to me! My saying is, if the dog bites you once, it's the dog's fault, but if he bites you again, then it's your fault.

And some people never make any change within their lives, ever. They walk around reliving their past and never grow up in their lives. I couldn't be them; it's a sad way to live. God wants more for us than we want for ourselves. He's living proof of that. I know I can pray for him or anyone else, but then they must want better for themselves as well, and most people don't. They talk a good game, but they aren't living anything, and they are waiting on the blessing of God to fall down on them. Then as I hear a preacher say: I guess they are looking for the pie in the sky or the magic lottery ticket as I heard another friend say, it's going to be his big break, but if you get Jesus, that's the biggest and best break for your life. I personally felt this person doesn't even believe in God. It makes our friendship hard because he told me that you believe in God and look at all the bad things that have happened to you! Well, I got something for that! It was grace that has kept me, and grace and mercy will keep me going.

Oh yes, I've been through a lot in the past 20 plus years that I've known him, but I'm an overcomer as well. When he's on the outside looking in, he sees the glass half empty, but if the grace of God falls in his life, he will see the glass half full as I know that God will fill it up in due time within my life according to His word and promise on my life for him. Now he's a police officer, and the covering that God has on his life is more than he could ever know.

He went to college to be a lawyer but ended up becoming a policeman. Now I think the shift change in his life was God. God put him where he needed to be. He's not the loving and caring type of person. He never shows any feelings about anything, but at the same time, he's never been married either. He's an only child and a strange guy in many ways. Nevertheless, I get along with him mainly because I understand him because I've put time into our relationship. He's not someone I would marry, never that, but we understand each other. A dose at a time. God puts all kinds of people in your path and for good reasons, and sometimes you might not even know why. Then years can go by, and you can indeed see the vision in them for you.

I've spent like I've said more than twenty years being his friend, and today I can see his value within my life. When God shows you the purpose of people in your path, you must respect your mind about them, and this happens more often than you can know. People can have great or little value, but the will of God for you with them will always stand out strong in your life. We sometimes miss the favor of God because we weren't looking for it, or it didn't come or happen the way we think it should. God has a masterful plan within His hands for us, and when things don't look like how we want, we think He has dropped the ball on us. However, we didn't know how to receive what He had planned for us because it didn't come the way we expected and missed it.

God's plan and our plans are not the same. And when we are looking for a favor from Him, we sometimes don't really know what to be looking for, but just trust that the plan of God for us is more than enough to carry us through. Giving grace unto Him with favor as we pray, keeps us standing in the midst of the storm. It holds us as we stand to push forward for the favor and the promise of God, not ever doubting Him but trusting in his Holy Word for the promise and favor; this is what keeps us going because without prayer, nothing happens in our life. For God likes praise, and as we praise Him, He releases favor. When I caught myself feeling so lonely and broken at the end of my avenge day, and I got home to the house that I live in and prepared myself for the close of my day and began to pray unto God for the blessing and shortcoming of the day's tasks, God will reveal so much to me that could have been but I missed it! People might have come in telling me the shortcoming of some story within their life, and I heard them but have much more to thank God for because that could have been me, telling that story about my child locked up or a death and the list goes on but favor, had me covered and my children as well. They don't take things as strongly as I do in Christ, but I know who's keeping who.

I can say: they ain't out there on drugs and so many more wrongful things that could be going on within their lives, but for every right, there is a wrong and none of us are perfect within God's eyes no matter what we may have or not have going on in our life. We all started somewhere. Well, we all end up somewhere as well. This is just food for thought because some of us put ourselves up to higher and better than others, but in God's eyes, we are all the same.

Money and color of our skin and the degrees we might have hanging on the walls are good, but He sees us all the same and putting on all the extras doesn't make us a bigger nor a better person than anyone else; just that we have been more blessed and favored in other areas than most, and sometimes these areas were not of us, but our family ties put before us. Some people never earned the title, let alone do the walk in their lives, and that shows as well. Sometimes, we have to stop and look in our past and future and figure out where we are going and understanding where we came from as well. This walk is crucial in life. I heard people say: the preacher's kids or PK's as they put it are the worst kids out there. Well, they were so busy with everyone's problems that they left their houses uncovered. This is so true because I've been married to some preachers and they are a mess at home. They say charity begins at home! If your house isn't in order, how are you going to get someone else's house in order? When they come down off the pulpit and take a look at their lives and family, it seems the whole message was for them.

Ministers preach to themselves first, but they aren't following what they are preaching either. Some of them are so full of themselves and the fact that they are men, enjoy all the attention the women give them running behind them and these aren't all single, but married men as well and the women are just as bad. Personally, I'm not moved by the foolish stuff that they do because I've been there and seen that.

I'm not moved by the lies but pray that they get it right, but I can't sit under the foolishness either and support the game when God has shown it to me. Sometimes you must be careful what you pray for. I asked God to show me, and I do believe that I might wish that I hadn't because I didn't like what I saw. It bothered me in my spirit for months. Then God gave me peace over it with much understanding. Understanding is the key to everything in our lives, no matter who's telling the story. They can call themselves any title that they like, but their lifestyle speaks for itself. And if you're truly watching, you'll see it for yourself, but if you don't, it's because they look just like you and you're in the game too. You can't see what you're not looking for. Why? Because you're doing it as well, and it's called playing a Christian when you're just churchgoers, and none of it will ever stand in the eyesight of God, ever! We must get the true meanings of the word of God inside us and not run behind anyone for any reason, but people do, and they aren't living within the will of God for their lives, and they will truly miss it.

The fashion show can't be because he looks good, or he sounds good, but you're still not getting anything out of it. I am not running behind the looks of a man or woman, but the true words of God to hit my spirit and conviction kicks in every time they open their mouth and when I get back to my corner of the world, I'm still dealing with the conviction from the past. If you're not, they ain't saying nothing, and you're not living anything but just call yourself doing who a favor? Nobody, nobody at all! This is such a big deal for God. Only what we do for Who? Christ will last! And that's that! If we put as much to serving God as we put into running behind men, we will already be alright right now. Don't chase fool's gold, people! Find your place in the ram of God and all the glory and promise of Him, and you'll be so much better than they look in front of you. I like to think that I'm not what someone might call pretty, but I do dress well, and I'm not dressed in what one they might call designer clothes. I do wear them, but the name is so small that you can't see it. People talk to me and throw out names of clothes, glasses, and whatever to me, and I don't know them. When they praise them, I keep saying if they were talking or praising God like they are praising and running to get the repeat of something that was out thirty or more years ago with somebody attaching a new name, well let's say they would be doing alright.

I can look good with giving my God the praise and glory as I walk. They get a moment at a time just like it flows off their tongue and - don't know them but live quite well off them, and they brag about what they wear and how much they are worth, and they live from paycheck to paycheck as they brag about them, who ain't putting nothing in your pocket but living wealthy off of you.

I have been similarly crazy before, and my children wore nice clothes. I gave them the best that I could, and today, I wish I had done things differently by them as well. Their children are being raised the same way they were, and the lack of respect in them shows too. They get caught up in the foolishness, and I know the times are much different, but people are not instilling anything of value into children today. The streets have them and the Gameboy or other video games. They don't jump rope and do silly stuff that we did as children. They have no unity in anything because it's designed to do everything by yourself, and that's wrong as well. It's in everything in the world today. There's no unity in the church first of all. People don't want to do anything together, and it shows so bad to me that sometimes all I want to do is run. In the schools, the teachers are fighting, and the kids are too. In the home, the parents don't have any unity other than if they sit next to each other at church watching their watch, timing their next move.

The kids see it, and they know what's real and what's not today, and on that note, how can that lead them anywhere? And I'm the same way, when I see so much, I must say they aren't leading me, and I'm not following them anywhere. Just for that reason, I'm careful about who is guiding me. And where they think we are going. God wants more for us than we could ever wish for ourselves. Then as we look around us and truly see what God has in store for us indeed within Him.

Then we have choices to make within our lives by ourselves, and it's all about us. Then as Christ becomes the Manager of our lives and starts taking control, only then the growth in Him comes forward for us.

I beseech you therefore, brethren, by mercies of God, that he present your bodies a living sacrifice, holy, acceptable unto God, which is your reasonable service. 2) And be not conformed to this world: but ye that he transformed by the renewing of your mind, that he may prove what that good is, and acceptable, and perfect, will of God. 3) For I say, through the grace given unto me, to every man that is among you, not to think of himself more highly than he ought to think: but to think soberly, according to as God hath dealt with every man the measure of faith.

4) For as we have, many members have not the same office: 5) So we, being many, are one body in Christ, and every one members one of another. 6) Having then gifts differing according to grace that is given to us, whether prophecy, let us prophesy according to the proportion of faith; 7) Or ministry, let us wait on our ministering; or he that teacheth on teaching; 8) Or he that exhorteth, on exhortation: he that giveth, let him do it with simplicity' he that ruleth, with diligence' he that sheweth mercy, with cheerfulness. 9) Let love be without dissimulation. Abhor that which is evil; cleave to that which is good. 10) Be kindly affectionate one to another with brotherly love' in honor preferring one another; 11) Not slothful in business; fervent in spirit' serving the Lord; 12) Rejoicing in hope; patient in tribulation: continuing instant prayer; 13) Distributing to the necessity of saints' given to hospitality. 14) Bless them which persecute you: bless, and curse not. 15) Rejoice with them that do rejoice, and weep with them that weep. 16) Be of the same mind, one toward another. Mind not high things, but condescend

to men of low estate. Be wise in your own conceits. 17)
Recompense to no man evil for evil. Provide things honest in the
sight of all men. 18) If it be possible, as much as lieth in you, live
peaceably with all men. 19) Dearly beloved, avenge not
yourselves, but rather give place unto wrath: for it is written,
Vengeance is mine; I will repay, saith the Lord. 20) Therefore if
thine enemy hunger, feed him' if he thirst, give him drink' for in
so doing thou shalt heap coals of fire on his head. 21) Be not
overcome of evil, but overcome evil with good.

-Roman 12: 1-21

There are times in our lives when we must make different types of sacrifices unto people that pass by us within our lives. There will be times when we might not want to help them because of our past relationship and things they did to us in our lives, and while we still have the hurting pain seeing them standing in front of us. However, everything that they might need help with while we are still holding on to the past is difficult, and all I can say is let go and let God take control of the task at hand. If we don't forgive and let go and let God take control, we can never grow. That includes growing in God's understanding or our own personality. Things can't move forward if we don't let go of the past. Our past is always going to be just that, and if we don't close the door, then we can't open a new one in life. God will transform all the *"its"* in our lives according to His will and then and only then the grace, mercy, and power of the Holy Ghost kicks in. I've seen the preachers, but I've never heard them speak in tongues unto God's anointing, and sometimes I think about the actions of them in different settings, and the little light goes off.

They dye their hair and beard to pull the younger women in the church, they are balding fast, but they won't share their heads, or some of them wear these new styles of wigs to keep up the look. The women are just as bad, and their list of vices gets longer. In these times, again, I'm looking for the anointing of God in it? God always gives you the renewing of minds at different times within our life, according to the task in front of us. The gift is given to the strong in Christ, and this is the time when you know who was called and who just went! It shows if you're looking at it because they can't hide it from you if you're a child of God.

Then you, if no one else knows who they are, and this is when your prayer life should be growing strong for the things you see but cannot change in others. I had a task put before me in the last few months. I told God that I would never let anyone live in my home again. I've been there and did that, and it never worked in my favor. Not because of money because I've had people live with me and never charge them one dime. But because if you're not faithful to God, then who? But anyway I did let someone come to stay with me for a while, and it wasn't them but me. First, I lied to

God and then myself because I said it will never happen again for no reason. My daughter had a new baby, and when she did, she wasn't homeless or anything like that, but because she hadn't had a child in more than twelve years, she stated she wanted to stay with me for a few weeks. Well, I said, no! I'm sure it hurt her even though she didn't say that, but you do know your children if you're in any kind of relationship with them.

My son had come to me the same day, and I replied no to him as well. Then I dropped the ball and went back on my word. Believe me; it's been so costly mentally because I had to try to make it seem right to me. You can lie to others, but when you lie to yourself, well, that's something else. So as I tried to make it seem good to me, I wasn't buying it at all.

As time passed by, I kept getting mentally sickened by the choices that I had made, and the funny thing about that the person staying wasn't doing much of anything, but the thought was what was eating at me. My statement to God for one and then my kids for two. Well, my kids, you can always say those magic words: they understand! But that's a statement to please you and you only because they never truly understand half of what we as parents say or do. The kids don't either but just deal with whatever is going on in front of them. But to know you just stood up and lied to God, that's something else. I believe that one of my husbands honestly thinks that he loves me.

His mouth says it all the time, but his actions are something else. When the statement is made, and I truly think about it, it burns me up on the inside! He couldn't because he has practiced ministry so long, he sells the stupid stuff to himself quite easily.

Then he walks around all the time in what one may call carefree, and in these times, I wonder, does he ever feel as I just told you how I felt about my wrongdoings? If he does, he never shows it. If his wrongdoing ever makes a difference, he never takes a form of remorse for his wrongdoing but continues to call it God's blessing, and if you know God and His works, then you know right from wrong because God is the first one to convict you on your actions.

Sometimes, it's so bad for me that I can't sleep until I get it right. My spirit isn't at rest, so my body gets no rest, and there's no peace in my mind regardless of where I am. When the grace and mercy of God kick in, and you have been convicted in Him, and you make peace with yourself because He's already forgiven you when it first happened, you got to go back and forgive yourself. We are always our worst enemy. Nobody can mistreat us as bad as we do ourselves.

I grant you this is not a religionist's thing but a part of the way God has built us. There is good and bad in all of us, but it takes a strong person to find fault in their own behavior and actions. At times, we feel that the challenge of the day was at its worst, and then something else happens. These times are when we start looking harder for the favor of God, which was always right there for the asking. These troubling times are when we should be continuing to have praise coming out of our mouth! The grace of God kicks in when the praise of Him is coming out. Mercy falls in many little forms in ways that we take for granted; then, we miss it. When others persecute us and drag our name through the mud, we are not supposed to get mad and cuss then but believe that God has our back and remain steadfast in His word.

I find this so hard sometimes because one can say: enough is enough, but the Word says that you must turn the other cheek. We are not supposed to question God's word about anything but just follow the straight road that was put before us. So, when people do wrong and say: God, please understand! Well, they say that because He and He alone gave us the word for a guideline for us to follow and put in place for such reasons, that's what He understands. And to please the flesh, I hate when ministers sugar coat the words of God to fit those people running with them to keep the church full. They know they aren't teaching what they were taught when they went to the church as a child, as they say: it was those old folks' way, but it is in the word also to bring up the child the way that it's supposed to, so when he gets old, he won't depart from the righteous path. Today, children aren't being taught anything good nor anywhere to go, and no one is truly leading them to a better lifestyle, and that's causing problems. There are problems because if they even go to church, in some cases, it's to get them out of the house and not for teaching the ways of Lord. In other cases, they aren't getting any guidance at all, unless it's the television or social media. And in most cases, somebody else is raising the children because they are in some kind of program like school, training, or sports such as dancing, basketball or others. In most of these cases, the parents aren't involved at all unless it's to drop them off and pick them up.

The church sometimes ain't much better for them too. Some churches run daycare centers and programs, which become a money-making network too. I've seen kids that really need help, but couldn't afford the program in the name of the Lord, so they were turned away. I've given money to such programs and then wished I hadn't got involved after I saw what was indeed going on in the House of God. They were stealing and doing everything. Wow, and all in the church, is this called ministry?

Then the ministries getting shut down for one thing or another, seems like a daily piece of bread from the outside looking in, and these are big names, doing big things, so they were saying, and I too, have sowed seeds into places, and then had my regrets as well. The bottom line, only what you do for Christ will last, and if I gave it from my heart, then I'm alright, but if it came out of my pocketbook, it wasn't worth anything anyway. Food for those who don't know, your pocketbook means nothing in the eyesight of God, but sure looks good in the church for those who like to brag about it, and it helps them look good too because they don't care where they get it from, just as long as they get it. Hint, hint? They don't care what's in your wallet as long as it gets in theirs as well, and they don't care where it's coming from? I heard a minister say, if you hit the lottery, don't forget to pay your tithes and offerings. This is a pulpit talk! Well, I've always felt that I didn't have to be in a car accident for God to bless me, but I hear that too all the time.

God doesn't have to hurt me to bless me, and I'm living proof of that one. I've been in more accidents than anyone I know, and I've never sued anyone nor received payment from anyone. I've always jumped out dancing unto the Lord and thanking Him for life after the accident. If God wants to bless me financially, it doesn't have to be in the numbers. I've seen so many homes broken up behind the lottery that it's unreal. I had a customer last week tell me her twenty plus years of marriage is coming to a close because she can't take it anymore.

All her husband does is to spend hundreds of dollars a day on the lottery. He owns a business but is draining it dry, and she had already helped to build it back up so many times and then got smart and found a job. Well, after the job, the husband quit on all the bills that he paid before. Everything fell on her shoulders, and he finds nothing wrong in it. He even tries to control the money that she spends on her uniforms. This is a special woman of God within all that she does. She walks the walk and indeed talks the talk. I'm not saying that anyone doesn't get fed up, but I suppose love has kept her there. A lot of times, we might have been tired years ago but yet hung on to our relationships. This is when you keep selling lies to yourself, but when you truly get fed up, you're fed up! I know that I personally have never had that gift of just putting up with men's foolishness, and it doesn't take much for me to say: that's enough.

I've sold that masterful plan to myself because it's not godly. And when we are so happy in the decisions that we make, that's the devil justified in his mess. The spirit of God has tolerance within all things, within our lives, if we are listening to Him. When the word says to turn the other cheek, well, we don't, and if we do, it's for a moment because the flesh brings it back up. When we should have tolerance, well at that moment as well because even if we aren't speaking it, we are feeling it in our hearts, and if we aren't careful, we show it in everything that we do. There are some feelings that we just can't hide. Walking in Christ removes the pain and heartache of the past and makes us strong to move forward. None of this happens in a day, but sometimes it takes years to heal. The healing process is just like the process that I'm going through right now from my motorcycle accident. I'm still trying to sleep with my foot elevated up on a pillow each night. I usually sleep on my side but now trying to sleep on my back. Not only on my back but also halfway up because my foot is hurt on the left ankle, my right toe, and part of the right side of my feet, and this is all on the left leg. Well, when I get up daily, it takes a moment before I can put pressure on my foot. But slowly, it comes back alive. Well, this is our daily walk in God's grace. It's a slow process, but it's going to get better, slowly but surely in your life. As you move forward, so does God; He moves forward with you. As you grow in Him, the grace grows in you.

As you keep Him first, the mercy of Him keeps you ahead of all of your life. It's that simple and straightforward. Well, I hear people say: they have this and that wrong with them, but it's been sixty years, and you say, you're Christian, and yet you've had no healing? How can you lead others when you haven't been delivered yourself? Leadership happens by example. When I speak of the healing of God, others around me have seen the healing and blessing that I speak of. They know how far God has brought me. They can walk up to me and give Him the praise of what they have seen God do in my life. This God, He's in action within our life, and this is when you know who you are running with as well. Every time something happens to me because things do, I just give it to the Healer. I don't run to the doctor when I know who I truly serve. They laugh at me, but I realize that's why they seem to be in somebody's office it sounds like weekly for something, so I know their faith is not where mine is, and they couldn't be doing all that praying they confess; because the power of God shows up in one's life and when they keep going through the same stuff all the time and don't realize that you're going to get the same result, well you're a fool. People do some foolish things in their lives. Sometimes it's the attention, but that's what they are looking for.

The whole walk that they put before you is an eternal lie, and they got you in it with them? They look for growth, but they have ruined it because the writing on the walls never washes away within some people's lives, and they don't even realize it because they blame everyone around them but never take responsibility for their own sins. How can they always put it on others but never their selves because they are in a comfort zone?

When my friend was telling me about her husband, I started thinking about the things that I've seen in him. Not ever sharing them with her but realistically, I see so much with him and her children, and she wanted more for them than they wanted for their selves. Over the years, I've seen her reach out to each of them spiritually and naturally. The task she put on her shoulders, I knew so well, not the same things but life problems in a marriage and different things with my children. My kids made life pretty easy for me because the biggest thing I asked for was that diploma.

Well, I got all of them. Then what they did after that was on them. Luckily they made good choices within their lives, and as a parent, a single parent, I was proud of them. Then, the choices they have made for them, let's say some of them were good and some of them were bad and didn't work within their favor, but as a parent, I've learned that I can't say anything to them, but I let them make the choices for their selves and trust that they make the right the decisions within their lives.

It sometimes hurt since I thought I was a good parent, but they say different. They charge me with the lack of parenting for working in spite of the decisions that I made as I was raising them, but through Christ, they still made it, and that's the grace of God. In the word when it says: rejoice with them when they are rejoicing and weep with them when they are weeping. I've found myself weeping more than rejoicing, and this is everyday life.

If we could turn all our bad in our life to our good, that would be great, but we can't because only what we do for Christ will last, and the rest is just our own ties that we get caught up in. We find ourselves so good at what we do wrong. The church is supposed to be the Hospital for the sick and wounded, in or out of Christ, but how can you help the wounded in Christ when you're wounded and not healed yourself? Then, if you've not reached the point of corrections in church, now where are we going? Nowhere! The statement that the doors of the church are open, but is it for the membership of the body of Christ in the numbers that they keep on the books, or is it for the healing and salvation of Christ to be pushed forward? I find in most churches whether large or small, it all adds up to be the same; if they get what they are looking for, they are happy and the person within the need, let's say mostly never gets delivered.

Then they leave the church, sometimes worse than they came in and turn their backs on God, but God had nothing to do with it at all but the works of the ones who put themselves before you with the master plan for themselves. You weren't in their plans, but what they thought they could get out of you until you were gone. It bothers me when I'm just an offering or seed to whatever they have going on but never gets a call beyond that. When I look at it, I must look at it in two ways.

One is in my heart and the second, my pocketbook. Of course, the love of God should flow over everything within our lives, and anything else shouldn't count, but they value their bank accounts and fill them out of yours. The right way is to let grace sometimes speak loudly in your mind. Then the love of God speaks to the heart, and your discussion kicks in on that moment what you're going to do. When I think of the goodness of God and His love within my life, these times freely flow within me. I know that no one could ever do the things that Jesus did, and He can't be replaced within anyone's life.

But I don't even try to make any comparison between God and myself. God did so much more than any person in the world can do, and I'm never trying to act as if I'm as good as Jesus or trying to fill his shoes. Many people mislead others into thinking they are God in so many ways, then when things don't go their way or the way they think it should be, they turn and put all the fault on God.

I don't understand why they put it on God when you're not in a relationship with Him. You spent your time chasing the ghost and then got caught up with the one put up in front of you. Grace allows us to see things differently at all times, regardless of who and where we are. Today, I had a customer trying to get her uniforms, and her kids, two daughters were trying to get to the pool. Well, she's trying to get work clothes, and all they are thinking about is that the pool closes at four-thirty. I had to get myself involved, as I usually do in everything and tell them.

The car that she was driving has a note, and the house has one too, and all you're worried about is the fun you're missing at the pool. Well, if she's out of uniform, it could cost her her job. Then where will you be living and maybe you'll be living on the bus that she was driving, that you're riding now. Food for thought: everything comes so freely and taken as such with the children, and it's the parents' fault, all the way. When I was raised, everything had a value to it. These days, everything has grades now like A, B, or F. Saying it lightly, there's always room for failure in one's life and action within their life as well. How we plan it is what comes out of it. The woman stated that God sent her in here today with her children to learn something from me, but honestly, I felt the lesson wasn't for them as much as for her. They showed me how controlling the girls are with her, and she didn't stop to correct them.

The oldest girl who was sixteen had more than a little bossiness in her with her mother. The ten-year-old didn't say much, and I took it to be her mother's spirit. She was soft-spoken and polite, as well. She never acted pushy to me, regardless of her time or mine when she shops. The oldest daughter must have the spirit of her father, and I guess he has a controlling nature. They say we are where we come from; it's in our DNA. Judging my kids, they are becoming more like me in many ways. They have never been bossy, not at all, that's me, alright.

Their father was and still is the quiet one, and when they are acting like that, that's him, and when they get mad and become too much to handle, oh, they are acting like their mother for sure. At least, that's how I used to be many years ago, and you can still pull that devil up in me if you push the buttons too much. I find myself praying to stay saved, always asking God to keep me near Him in all things. Work can be tiring at times, and I can't wait for the day to end, but that's not often. Usually, I enjoy my job and can't wait to get there in spite of anything else. This is my safe haven, and I love my job. Helping people is glorified in my work because I'm first looking out for them, and I guess one might say we make each other's day. I don't think that people don't get mad at me sometimes when I won't let them have their way with me. I am like, oh well, they will get over it. And usually, they do because they come back and tell me how they felt and still shop with me. Sometimes, you don't need a mirror to look at yourself; just look at your children. They will show you who you truly are in more ways than one. You can watch them, and if you're looking close enough, they will bring tears to your eyes, even when they aren't around.

When you think about some stuff, and it's just you in that quiet place, and when they aren't around, and you're all alone, they'll never know because you don't share your heartbreak with them, ever. This is the time when in the Word, it says: when your enemy is hungry, feed them. It may be your family or fake friends, and you still stay in arms reach for them, regardless of whatever they might have done or taken you through.

The promise of God steps in and picks up in spite of them for you because you're still carrying the pain of yesteryears and walking side by side with them too. This is when the evil in people turn over for your good in Christ, and you don't have to say one word. They already know, and they will never say a word either, but the outcome is different for both the involved parties. Christ got you, and conviction got them. Look at God's glory, falling down on us with mercy and grace to follow every step of the way. When God's mercy for us fills one's life, everything takes a shift change, and it all begins in the mind and heart of man. When the Word says: so a man thinks, so is he. I told a young lady about weight loss today. Mostly, I wanted her to start loving herself and put the cigarettes down. Weight loss begins mentally before physically in one's life. You can do all the quick stuff out there in the market, but as soon as you stop, the weight comes back. I just know that smoking is bad, and she said it replaced food, but what does the word speak on that!

God designed us perfectly, and He said certain things about eating as well. I suppose God's plan was designed to work for our good, and man's plan is to destroy people everywhere. There's so much stuff being sold to people, which is no good for the body that it is unreal, and people can't see it. They drink or smoke it, and the list goes on. Some of the things they say are all-natural, but I can say: when it's all-natural, that's when it comes straight off a tree or something like that.

When it's made in a pill or liquid form, then it's no more natural and the way that God made it. It was good and the way man transformed it, it's a good selling point for him. The market is overflowing with *"get rich"* quick schemes and multiple players as well, and they get you sold on it so hard that nobody can tell you anything. That's in real estate and everything else. Drinking water is their biggest game. More than five hundred brands are present, but God is the only one who made water. They recycle it and sell it back to you over and over again. Little more of this and less of that and stick a name on it, and people run to buy it quicker than praising God for it. The only name I push so hard is the name of Jesus because it's the greatest name I know, and so where else is there for me to go? The rest you can wear and push them, but what have they got to offer back to you honestly? Nothing, nothing at all, but they look good on you. I would guess that's what I hear out of your mouth and see on your back.

I have a problem trying to figure out who's who; because they are all starting to walk, talk, and dress, and the list goes on like that, especially in the church. They got fan's titles and who knows what else, and they are pushing it so hard, but it's not the words of God, just the words of people. When I see it, I grab my purse, run, and don't look back. With some of them I find that association is everything and that on any given day, I just don't want any part of it.

I found myself trying to help someone and realize that the way I was thirty years ago, I'm still that way today. It was the virtue instilled in me from my parents, and I've never dropped the ball. Well, I had to go back on my word with them because the strong way that I had been taught was still there, and I couldn't do what they wanted from me, I guess when the word says: raise the child the way it should go, when they get older, they won't depart from it. I found it was true because over fifty years later, I'm still stuck on *"that ain't right, and I can't do it."* Today, those types of parents are gone, but what was instilled in me is still standing strong. God put everything in order for us to follow but left it up to us to keep it upright before Him at all times within our lives. For example, have you had a time in your life when you were doing or saying something that you just knew was wrong, but yet you continued to move ahead and then said God forgive me? Well, He knew it before you did it and that God forgives you, but where was the spirit of God before the act? You go to Him to ask for forgiveness when you could have done things differently, but He still forgives you.

Now, did you forgive yourself? Well, generally, we find contentment within ourselves and think since we went to God each time, they weren't doing something out of order, and it's okay. I believe not because He gives you a reprobated mind, and you get eternally lost from God. Free will is dangerous. People often misuse the word of God for their own purposes. And they justify everything bad to be good and fixed in Jesus without the commitment of a shift change within their life. I do believe God can make a change in some of our lives at the door of the dead.

The reason I know that is, I asked for another chance there. He gave it to me, and sometimes, I feel as if l am not where I should be in Christ and immediately began praying for help in the area that I find myself slipping in. Most of the time, we all can help correct what's going on if we aren't strong enough to do it for ourselves, we can always go to the Father, He's always there for our asking, but generally, we don't ask, do we? When I hear songs with verses like He's the Father for the fatherless and the Mother for the motherless, I feel as if they were written just for me. You don't always realize what you truly have until it's gone. The loss of my parents played a vital role in my life daily. They passed years ago, and sometimes, it seems as if it was yesterday, and I do realize that they are always still in me and within me in the spirit ram of my life.

Taking grace or mercy makes the difference within one's life. If your relationship with them was good and you have a clean heart about them, it's not that you can't miss them but will enjoy the moments within your heart and mind that you had with them. If you did things out of order to them, you're going through something else with thoughts about them disturbing you after they pass away. We all are only here for a short while, and what we do with the time that we are here is something else. The controls are in our hands for our lives, and we must use them to make wise choices in our lives. Some people are not going ever to do that.

They stand on the pulpit speaking the words of God but live something else all the time. I heard the freaks come out at night, but I also heard, what's done in the dark will come to light. I just went through something just like that. They were speaking one thing but doing something else, and I'm sure they think I don't know the difference, but I do and not saying anything because it's not my place. But the God I do serve has your name and address, and He and He alone has control over all things within one's life. The glory of it all is in Him, and I'm not mad but crying, crying for you, not me! Crying out to God in the spirit ram for deliverance within your life for you.

Again, sometimes people could want more for you than you want for yourself, but because you don't acknowledge the wrongdoings within you, you think nobody sees you, but they do; you think nobody knows, but they do, and they aren't talking to you about your improvement, but to anyone who will listen about you and when I hear it, instead of dragging you through the mud, I drag you to the Lord in prayer because I know that is the only thing which brings hope for you in your mess. What does it take to keep up doing wrong when one could just do the right thing? Is it better to sleep on and wonder why you stay sick all the time and can't sleep at night because your sins are eating at you all the time? You can always stop and say: I want to get it right.

There is no hope for a brighter tomorrow because you did nothing different today. No rest tonight because you closed no old sin's door and didn't open a new shift change in your life. And no God and no peace in your actions. To find God is to find peace and more than that to get everlasting happiness within one's life. It matters from the beginning of one's life to its outcome that the choices one makes within their lives are correct. All lives do matter in Christ. Last night, I had the pleasure of meeting a friend that I've had for sixteen years. I had this old friend meet me at a restaurant where my son and a girlfriend of mine were having dinner. Well, when my friend came in, he hugged and kissed me. My son replied to him that he had never seen that before, he said I've known my mother longer than anyone at the table, and she doesn't hug and kiss. Well, my friend felt awkward about the statement that my son had made.

Later, after I had reached home and my son was gone, my friend spoke about the comment that my son had made. My reply was, for the most part, it was true, but in the past sixteen years that I've known him, I've also made some shift changes within my life, and learning to let people hug and kiss me was one of them. Now, people don't look for a change in anyone, especially when they aren't looking for any change within you. The statement made me feel bad, not because it wasn't true because it was, but because I truly hadn't been a loving person in my life to anyone, including my children. But God has changed my heart to some degree about my actions within my life. I'm not saying I've been truly delivered because I haven't. I know I still have a long way to go in Christ, and I'm a continuous piece of work in process. God grants us our heart's desire if we give in to Him. We must realize that the problem is there and make the first move towards fixing it.

God takes care of the rest because He is that helping hand in all things to those who love Him, but first, we must start loving ourselves. Looking over the moment with my son last night and he said so much more that I'm not saying but allowing it to run around in my mind and do some thinking about me and not him. He's thirty-nine years old, not thirty-nine years young, and I can't undo what was already done nor fix it in his heart for me or mind that. However, I can respect his mind for the things that came out of his mouth with love and understanding of where he was in life with me.

This is not him but each of my children in different ways and my grandchildren as well. They all have specific views about me, and they know what I like and dislike because I make it a point to express that to them. But I also see where I should have been handling things entirely differently with today's experience. For the children, well, it's too late. There is still some hope for me in my grandchildren to understand a different me.

I've been pushing them away as well, and they say: that's just the way I am but not because I do it so much to them, but because their parents taught them that, and I haven't tried to make it any better for them. Then, we can allow ourselves just to accept things as they are but never try to go back and fix it. Now I have a new mission; it's called get it right before God and man. Getting it right is easier said than done because I must work at it daily. No, I don't see them daily, nor do I talk to them, but just because they are out of sight doesn't mean that they are out of mind.

Your mind will never stop running as long as you live, and the things that go across it are a mess within. Then when you put new things on it to think about, there are times they don't even let you sleep thinking about them. Then the actions are harder because you don't honestly know where to start, but remember that you got to start somewhere. That's when God's little mercy stop by your room to guide you on the new journey in front of you, with His love to hold you through the task now in front of you.

No, your family or others aren't trying to receive it, you must see the shift change because they aren't looking for it in you, so they see no good in you, but just the wrong that they had before in their hearts for you. It's going to take so much more effort from you to get the right message across to them while they grieve themselves to death with the hurt and pain of their life trials.

I know this would never be me to death, but there are times I grieve the shortcoming in my life in terms of my family and so-called friends because I want more for them than they want for themselves? They don't see it, and I don't even speak it out loud but unto the Father of fathers Who is the only one Who first knows my heart and hears my prayers and wipes my weeping eyes within these hard times. It is the time for people in all their mess to let go and let God restore and take control within their lives for the worthiness of Him is everything. These are truly the times that we must have a hand up in Christ within our lives and ensure He is in control of our good. Blessing in one's life comes in so many ways that we can't truly miss it! God's grace falls the same way as well. We want to always give thanks in everything, whether good, bad, or indifferent.

While taking a moment to check my motherhood again, now as I honestly think about it; back then I thought that I was right in my actions with my children, but today, one can say I was so wrong in so many ways that I was overall more wrong than right. Forgiveness is hard to come by for anyone. It doesn't matter who, but our guard is up high, and the Christ is down low. They say they know God and live unto Him, but their actions speak something else. They never release the hurt and pain of life with forgiveness, and this is from the pulpit on down. Not only do others see it, but you also feel it in their message because it's always so personal, and if you hear their story, you realize that there always are repetitions. There are different Sundays on the calendar and different year as well, but they go through the same pain over and over again. They never leave their past, so they keep dumping it loud and clear, and they never get over it! God can't release to you what you never let go and let Him have it! The ones they give it to, can't help them at all, and they lose more than they gain. And that's sad because the ones who care are now gone. Sometimes, people flee for different reasons, especially in the church! Some money-hungry preacher has run them away with their begging.

Others run them away with their hoeing around down the front of the pulpit. They like the young women chasing them, and then they sleep around with them. This includes both men and women as far as gender goes. Then the church members run like I'm doing now. How many wives or men can one have in one church? My answer is as many as you play the game with.

But I'm not a true player because I can't do it, and I know God knows who I am, and when they realize, then they will too if they know God with sincerity. God shows us everything good in our lives, but if we don't appreciate Him, then it's no good. He again wants more for us than we want for ourselves. Taking it to another level in life is our personal growth, so we can see things differently, and then things change swiftly as well.

God keeps us according to the word of God in our lives, and this always makes the difference between the churchgoers and the true Christian who believes in Christ. Christ always shines bigger and brighter to those who truly love Him. Growth always comes to those who serve Him with favor. God required little from us, but we expect more of Him in our life.

The wage of sin is death when we don't live according to the Word. Some people walk around doing everything wrong under the sun as if the Godly rules don't apply to them at all. Well, I guess if they think they are preaching and say that they work in Christ, then they are okay, but what does the word say. The things that they say they are doing right don't erase the wrong they do unless they get it all right with God.

It doesn't make sense to stand up and preach something you're not living yourself under no circumstances, but want people to follow what you say! I find it in a lot of churches that this goes on, and most people don't notice it because they aren't with Christ where they should be, but running behind the person standing before them and make them their god. I'm not that person, and I always ask God to show them to me in reality for who they are. When you see it, then you know it for yourself, and that should be enough. I hear people talk about the one standing before them, but you still run behind them, and for the life of me, I don't know why they are talking about them, but their actions speak something else

89

about them and you as well. If I firsthand knew something about someone, I couldn't take part in it. I could pray that they get it right unto God, but not continue to run with them because they are wrong, and then you play a part as well. It's one thing not to know, but it's something else to know and still hang strongly with them in their wrongdoings, as that makes you no better than them. We all have some ways in which we can improve in our life. We do some things wrong, yet don't take knowledge of our wrongdoings, but if we know, that's something else in God's eyesight.

There are times in our life when we must be responsible for all that we do. That may be here on earth or the judgment day with God, but we will have to answer at some point, and I just feel God is not going to understand when we try to make Him understand the wicked ways that we had. How can they defend while they were teaching something else before people? God wants us to practice what we preach.

But preaching while not practicing is something else. God's grace within one's life is like a bright light not at the end of the tunnel, but completely illuminating through the tunnel. He keeps the warning signs and shows us small signs to guide us if we are listening if not even looking. Thinking hard on things in my past, all I can say is, thank you, Lord, for keeping me. I make it a point to tell people the shortcoming that I see within them, as I saw them within myself. Not to be rude but because somebody got to say something to help each other in today's times. Everyone is going through something, but they are not talking to each other, and as I always hear, there are more rumors than facts. People don't trust due to the fact they shared stuff with someone, and then they heard it again. I was told that something I shared with a preacher, he went and said to the people in a bible study what I shared with him. At this time, I had never been to his church, but I did visit sometime later, and it was more than a year later that some of the members shared things with me that he had said that I told him.

They found it to be funny, but I had to take a hard look at the person. For one, how can you be a preacher, a man of God, but can't hold water if I put it in a glass and hand it to you! Then if you did this, I'm surely glad that I didn't share any more than I already had, and definitely won't be sharing anything else with him. Where is the trust in the pastor if you can't go to them then to whom? I've known pastors for twenty years, and I've shared all kinds of stuff with them.

I visit their church all the time and not once has anyone ever came back and said anything that I've shared with them. They have played important parts in my life when I have had to go to a minister for help or, if nothing else, an ear for the things that I might have been dealing with. This pastor is a wonderful woman of God. She prophetically spoke of things in my life, and they happened just like she said they would.

One time my husband and I had taken a trip to Virginia, and when we got off our flight, I received a phone call that my son had been in an accident in the mountains of North Carolina. Well, I called her, and she told me to go back and get a flight back home, and when I arrived home, call her back, and God will have given her the answer for what's next. When I arrived home, I called her, and she said to take three cars to pick up my family. My mother, my sister, and I drove up there because she said God told her that He was sending all my family home, but they needed room to be comfortable for the ride home. Well, my oldest son had a broken arm and collar bone, and glass had gone in his eyes.

My youngest son, who fell asleep at the wheel, had less stuff wrong with him, but he was still messed up as well. Maybe the grace of God was in his life as a minister himself was covering him. Then my granddaughter was in a full-body cast, and her mother had her spine messed up. When my son fell asleep, the truck went off the road and hit a tree. It started flipping, and as it flipped, everyone was thrown out of a window.

My granddaughter went out of the window, while still in her car seat when they found her by someone who was passing by and saw my son crawling to the side of the road for help. If that child of God hadn't been able to do that, and if the truck had gone off the cliff, we would have never known what happened to them. But praise be to God, His grace and mercy protected them even in a time like that. Some people don't understand the favor of God and the power within Him for guiding our lives. Well, let's say I do. And when I was taking pictures of them, they said, *"Ma, why are you taking pictures of us hurt like this?"* Well, today, I still have the pictures, and I tell them to look at the grace of God. Today, they are all healed by the power of God and the favor that He had upon them all of their lives.

In memories like these all I can say is, thank you, Lord, for you have been so good to this family, and I know that some of them are missing it because they aren't yet serving the Lord as they should, as they are still caught up in their own sins, and that they justify being right but are only right to themselves. God's grace covers families just like mine all the time, and most people miss it. I try not to take the grace of God for granted in my life. I know that I, too, have been in the same place because I have also missed the grace just like everyone else, but it's not in my heart to overlook the blessing of God in my life.

He brought me so far, and I've got my future to go as well. None of us is perfect, but some people play all the time perfectly, and then some of the things that they say and do will surprise you because they never check out their personality in the mirror. They only see one way and believe that it's truly the right way. God shows us ourselves without a mirror directly in our hearts and minds.

Our thinking is a guide map to our lives, but our actions can become the path of destruction in someone's life. We and only we can continue to stay off track because we want to, instead of getting it right when we get the warning of God in our spirit ram. God holds out His loving hand in times when we think He's not there, but He always is. My family didn't heal in a day or a week, but it took months of healing; however, things could have been much worst. My oldest son's friends made sure he didn't lose his business. They gave money and support in every way that they could.

Today, he still speaks of the favor that they showed in friendship to him in so many different ways. This son is just like his father; he gives away more than he will ever get back in so many ways. I sometimes get mad when I see people just using him on every level they can, but then again, I know both of his parents are that way too. He sometimes reminds me of things that I've done as well, and then you can't say anything but check your memory.

You must say, oh well, that's true and keep moving forward because you know who you were as well. Most of the time, I try to give back to the ones that I know have a true need in their businesses. Everyone that cries broke isn't broke but doesn't want to spend their money on what makes their money in the first place. Talking about being stupid, I see them every day, and I look at the car they might be driving or the purse they are carrying; then I just shake my head at them and ask the big question: why do you support things that put nothing in your pocket but takes it out from it, but your uniform that you need to make your money with, you don't want to buy it but keep that car and house? That's crazy to me, but it's their choice. When we continue to walk and talk to God, all the things that used to be so important in our lives just don't matter any longer because He becomes that car, that house, and the pocketbook.

You get so full of Him and less of people that use to fall so freely off of your tongue. He's the replacement for all the stuff that you probably didn't even need in your life. It becomes all of Him and none of them. They steal away the joy and love and everything else when you make others your God. If it's the pastor, you're missing it; if it's your car, then it's the same thing; and sometimes, it can also be the people you hang around with as well, you're missing all of the grace because God's not in it at all.

You will get no peace of God this way. Remember, He can bring the joy of the world at your fingertips all the time if you serve Him when the shift change comes in, and the lust of the flesh passes away. My flesh was busy, too, not with men but with shopping. I used to think that I had to be kind to me every day. Well, today, God is good to me every day of my life because I go to sleep with Him on my mind. When I wake up, He's still there, and as I move daily, He is still there. I thank God for His grace and mercy on my life as I walk with Him daily. It makes me feel good when a stranger that has never come to my job before tells me they feel the spirit of God on me. Well, they say you know the spirit, and then they speak prophetically into my life. I know it is the voice of God using them because they don't know me from anywhere else, but they know God, and He knows me. These are times when I look back, and people speak things to me and say God said it, but I don't feel it in my spirit that it came from God, and then later, it shows that it wasn't indeed from Him as well. God doesn't lie, but men do.

If He says it will come true which might not be in a day, it's going to happen because God said so, and it's always done. The timing is not always to our liking, but according to the Lord. Remember, things will always happen in His timing and not ours. God has gotten me, and I pray that He has you too. Prayer changes things, but with praying, you need the actions of one's self in faith as well.

Time and again, we cut ourselves short from God's grace and mercy. Yesterday a family member of mine asked me to join other family members for dinner. Well, I declined for the lack of trust. I've been out to those dinners, and for one, I don't eat much anymore, and I cooked almost everything that I had to eat today. For two, I was wondering who is paying for the food, probably my oldest son! Then three, why would I go out with people who don't respect me? Four, I'm not fake and can't fake the move, even though the family member let's get together sometime other than a funeral. Well, a funeral is a family reunion for me.

I live daily, and no one ever calls to say hello, but if they have a need, then I hear from them. Since I quit doing handouts, I don't hear from distant relatives because I don't supply the free lunches anymore, but my son does, and that's alright with me. But I won't be a part of the big show, and the more you invite, the greater the bill for him, so I'll pass. It's sad always to see the worst in things, but my dad gets the credit for that one in me.

He said if they always borrow money from you but never pay it back, then when you see them ask them first before they hit you up. I've found this to be so true, and the look on their faces tells the true story of how they felt. Somethings you can't hide, and facial looks are one of them. They are worth more than you can ever imagine. God's grace is always the same in all situations. All I can say is that His grace is more than enough for me.

23) *Take heed unto yourselves, lest ye forget the covenant of the Lord your God, which he made with you, and make you a graven image, or the likeness of anything, which the Lord thy God hath forbidden thee. 24) For the Lord, thy God is a consuming fire, even a jealous God. 25) When thou shalt beget children, and children's, children and he shall have remained long in the land,*

and shall corrupt yourselves, and make a graven image, or the likeness of anything, and shall do evil in the sight of the Lord thy God, to provoke him to anger: 26) I call heaven and earth to witness against you this day, that he shall soon utterly perish from off the land whereunto ye go over Jordan to possess it, he shall not prolong your days upon it, but shall utterly be destroyed. 27) And the Lord shall scarred you among the nations, and he shall be left few in number among the heathen, whither the Lord shall lead you. 28) And there ye shall serve gods, the work of men's hands, wood, and stone, which neither see nor hear nor eat nor smell. 29) But if from thence thou shalt seek the Lord thy God; thou shalt find him, if thou seek him with all thy heart and with all thy soul. 30) When thou art in tribulation, and see all these things are come upon thee., and even in latter days, if thou turn to the Lord thy God, and shall be obedient unto his voice; 31) (For the Lord thy God is a merciful God;) he will not forsake thee, neither destroy thee, nor forget the covenant of thy fathers which he sware unto them.

-Deuteronomy 4: 23-31

When we are listening to and walking in the anointing of God, we must be totally committed to God. He's a powerful God and will not have any other God entertained other than Him. Now we can turn anything that we love or misuse into our personal God.

I liked to shop too much, and it came easy because my mother and father did the same thing. They both had different interests, but in God's sight, it was all the same. My father was a man above men who loved tools, cars, and trucks. My mother was a woman who took great pride in her clothing, fabric, and sewing and wasted as much as my father did with cars. Well, now take my case, I overdo all of the general cursed things that were passed down the family tree. The reason I say that is because my grandparents were just like my parents, and my kids are not any better.

We waste too much on everything that we touch. It's all a sin in God's eyes, and to be wasteful when others are going through tough times isn't right. Now, I used to say that the poor will be with us always because the word of God says so. I later learned that wasn't any reason for me to be wasteful. God didn't respect me doing it, and I don't give people things that I don't want. I try to treat them as I treat myself in so many ways. No, it's not equal, not at all! But if I felt it was trash, I threw it in the garage.

If I wouldn't wear it, then I wouldn't give it away. If someone asked me for it, then it was a different story. God's the same way. He wants the best for us as well, but we don't want it for ourselves. God doesn't quit on us, so we shouldn't give up on Him either. We must keep ourselves away from the sins of the world daily. They are real and just waiting for a new soul to attack, which can be yours. Satan has nobody until he gets yours, and no face until you give him yours as well. God only keeps who wants to be kept. If you say you can, you will, and if you say you can't, then you never do! It's that simple, and we can control our lives that easy with Christ on our side. When my parents died, I looked at all the stuff that they left for someone else to clean up behind them. I made up in my mind then that I'll clean up my mess by myself. I'm no better a packrat than my parents, and all of their children are the same as well. Let's say practice makes perfect; that's us.

We are all nasty hoarders. Don't go into that closet, and you'll be fine, but if you touch that door, then oh well, you don't know what might fall out on you. Today, I wore the skirt that I wore twenty years ago when my youngest son graduated high school. I can still fit it, but my weight is more now than it was back then. It probably has been moved fifteen times, and now my stuff is packed up in storage. Somethings I say I'm going to get rid of, but memories are something else.

We can't always cut them, but we find a reason to keep holding on to the things that we want due to the memories. This is our everyday life, as well. We can't forget what people did wrong to us as well as the good times. Mainly, it seems we have more bad than good on our plate. Have you ever met a family member that you haven't seen in twenty years? Instead of asking about some of the good things that happen in your life, they start asking you something foolish about that cookie your mother said not to eat, and she whipped your behind when you were ten years old. Well, you were ten then and since then went to college, and you're a teacher now. But they haven't moved beyond that whipping you got when you were ten. This is because people, regardless of who they are, don't look for the good in you or anyone else.

They love the bad in everything. This is why I don't look at the news. Five minutes of good and the next twenty minutes of bad, who needs to feed that to themselves. But millions do and then worry about things that aren't in their control, and nothing that they can do about it anyway. However, it keeps them talking about it all day or even all week long. They live for it, and they wonder why they age so quickly because of what they feed their spirit, and they can't change, but they live for it anyway. God gave us the Bible as our guide to follow. Millions of people don't use it for guidance, but can't wait to get in front of the television set. Then they call others to bear witness if they saw the news as well.

However, they don't spread the word of God the same way, but they will talk about church gossip that way. I've seen many times when I haven't even arrived home, and my phone is ringing off the hook with stuff like that! Did you see that dress she had on, and did you hear that lie the pastor told in the pulpit today, and then they say we know that was a lie! Well, we might both know that, but you're only talking about it to me to run back with me to them.

And then when I hear it again, guess what, it is like I was doing all the talking and you were doing all the listening. Well, I don't think so because that's not honestly how it went, but I don't care about any of it. This is when I say oh my God, and He knows the genuine truth about all things at all times, both in and out of the church, even when you don't realize how out of order you are, which is something else.

When the one standing before you talk as much about the business of others, you don't expect any more from the members because leadership is by example; and that's the example put before them by the preacher because they run together, and it's nothing to them but service and gossip as usual. What does God think about all of it? I'm sure he's not pleased, and they wonder why I don't entertain but walk on by them because I've seen them in action. Then they step down off the pulpit with a nasty attitude and say they are leaders. Well, I think not, and I can't find that their actions within the actions of Christ in their lives because they show something different.

And it's not the actions and spirit of God. My God is an unchangeable God. He stays the same, today and tomorrow, and forevermore. When the Word says: you know the spirit by the spirit, you do if you have it, and you know when it's not of God as well, and God doesn't dwell in an unclean temple. They went to get the ones who don't know any better, and since I know better, I don't follow them but flee and flee fast from them. I had a member of the church call me up and talk nasty to me about Father's Day. Well, he's not my father, and I felt that I don't behave like a hypocrite for any reason. I don't talk to you on a daily basis. So I didn't call them on Father's Day, and I guess they felt it in an insulting way. Well, when I received the call and the manner it was in, I was shocked because I didn't think it was that serious. Some people think it's all about them, well it isn't!

My father is gone, and I can't say I was grieving him because I've never grieved my parents at all, but nevertheless, I felt it was too much. Why didn't he call to see why I wasn't in church today? Oh, because he didn't have to because someone told him that I was home, cleaning my closet. Well, I was, and I felt the need was more important to me than the big show at church for Father's Day.

Maybe since my father is gone, and I have a lot on my plate and things that I might need to do at my house, and something I must take care of myself, I did, and I don't have to explain that to anyone. God knows my heart, and He also knows that I work six days a week, and Sunday is my only day off. I usually don't miss church at all. Some Sundays, I'm in two or three churches because I give my job all my time daily, and when Sunday comes, I give the Lord the best of me on that day. I don't get tired of going to work or church because I don't quit on God, as I don't want Him to quit on me either. I pray: Lord, can I get up and go to work in the morning? And each day I do, and I'm always there for Bible study and Sunday services when people tell me about them. So for this man to confront me like that, it was uncalled for when I have never seen him on time for service. He is never in Sunday school and always late for the services when he does come, and he finds nothing wrong with that. Yet, he's trying to correct me! Leadership by example and the example that I see here, I can't follow, and that's all too much for me. People make up all kinds of reasons to justify their actions. His reason is, he lives so far, but I feel so do I.

I drive an hour just like him, and I still come, but nobody appreciates that! They think I got it like that, but they don't know my story and are always trying to lead me, but to where? Nevertheless, the God I serve knows my heart first, and then He and He alone is the only one that I'll answer to and who can judge me as well. You don't know a man until you have walked in his shoes. This is so true. I can remember when I couldn't bathe myself to go to church, and today I can. I remember when someone had to dress me, but today I live by myself, and there are clothes that I can't zip and stuff like that.

So if I can't zip it, I wear it under the jacket unzipped so that I can get out of it when I get back home; but I still keep moving, and if somebody still talks crazy to me, all I can do is pray for them because they got a life all twisted. And it's not for me to help straighten them out, but let them get with Jesus because I can't do anything for them. They find themselves always calling me to get me straight but never listening to the fact that I had a real man for a daddy, and he has already raised me, and I'm not looking for a new daddy because there was nothing wrong with mine. He wasn't a crack head or anything but a businessman and a very smart one at that, and I'm walking in the anointing of him daily. Then sometimes he says stupid stuff to me, but I don't even reply because it doesn't deserve an answer, not at all.

But he thinks I'm a fool telling it to me, so I listen but know that I'll never follow his lead because he's not trying to lead me anywhere, but to the poor house by following him. I got this far by listening to my parents, and the guidance that they put before me was to work for the things I want in life. That's why I'm still working and plan on doing that for many more years to come because it's what I know how to do, and I do it well. My customers love me and look forward to me serving them. I love them, and I'm a faithful servant of God; all I want is to get up and get to them in the morning.

God's grace gets me there each day, and His mercy keeps me there as I've been working there for more than one-fourth of my life, and that's all I care to do besides serving God. God's grace has put me back together and keeps me moving forward in Him. Today, it's all about Jesus and not me. For the grace and mercy of

Him is everything in my life. I've been through the storms, and I've been dunked under the water and dragged through the mud, and the list goes on, but God had bigger plans for my life. Today, all I want is to continue serving Him with all that's in me, and when the snares of life approach me, I now will stand still and wait on God. I know He has gotten me covered. I know that anything else will not work in my favor. I realize who has control in my life. And the greatest of all, He and He alone loves me. Others say they love you, but it's a one-way street. They like what you can do for them. They are takers, not givers, and they are there just for their own selfish reasons in your life. I've seen it over and over again in people's lives and the pain that it causes as well.

Today, I just look to Jesus, and that's enough for me because I know He will never fail me, but the men of flesh will. They lie as good as a carpet, and they give you what they think you want to hear. They never take a break because they sell the same lies to themselves as well. They believe in their own mess, and giving it to you comes easy if you're listening to them. I try not to see or hear foolishness from them if I can help it. This makes my prayers real strong.

I weep for them as well, and they think I'm crying for me; in fact, I'm crying for them to get it right before it's too late. I can't even stand to hear some people's voices because you never hear anything but their bossy way and cold behavior. You know they go to church, but never feel and see Christ in them. You have tried to befriend them but also know that it's not going to ever happen for them because of the evil in them. The evil shows everywhere they go, and when people ask you about them, you are speechless.

Not sometimes, but at all times, if you don't have anything good to say, don't say anything at all, and that's how I handle most people who I come across. Sometimes at work, I know the spirit when it walks in the door. I might say leave and never look up, but the spirit of God lets me know they shouldn't be here, and sometimes they are customers, and all they want to do is give me a hard time for no reason at all, and all I want is to get them out of there.

Then there are the customers that say: I came in and planned to spend three hours with you, and I say: not today, I don't have time for you because I got other stuff to do, but they stay anyway, and that's the love of God in one's heart. Sometimes, they get mad if I'm not talking their heads off. We join hands in prayer too. Sometimes, they only come by to get me to pray with them or for them as well. I never ask what they need, but go straight to Jesus because He already knows, and I just give it back to Him.

When you go to get prayer, I believe that you should speak it in the open air. The devil is listening and waiting to get in your way, between God and you. I just say, Father, you already know what they need and release it unto them. It's not openly in the air but still from your heart unto God's ears. And He and He alone is the keeper of your prayers. You can tell others what you want and see what it gets you. All your business in the church and streets aren't going to help you any more than just talking about you.

These are times you find out who's a Christian and who only goes to church; who's your friend and who isn't? Everything has the good, the bad, and the ugly, and you got to know when and who you're talking to. I sometimes tell people that I know gossip stuff because I know they can't keep anything from people.

It's funny because they tell it to who I wanted to hear it. Well, I wouldn't say it myself, but they still got it. I know this is wrong, yet I do it, and I'm not going to make up an excuse for it either. God knows I'm wrong, and so do I, and I have to ask God to remove this bad spirit from me because when you do wrong and know it, you know who's using you.

The devil from the pit of hell! And if you don't get it right, that's where you'll end up with him, and I'm not trying to go there at all. You can't say God knows, but then don't do anything to correct your actions, either. That's wrong, and God knows that too. Then I hear the scripture: only what you do for Christ will last. But only what you do in Christ will last as well, and when you're out of Christ, you know that as well, and you'll have to answer for that.

It doesn't take much to find ourselves out of the will of what God says and wants for us. We do it so easier, and sometimes people try to compare themselves to what was written in the Old Testament, and that's why the New Testament was written for correction within our lives. But so many leaders of God try to live as Solomon did but forget what God said to correct them. That was then, but we should have a better understanding and living method for today's times to ensure the guidance of our lives today decently. I try to live according, and when I run into the ones who live in any kind of different way, I flee from them. I don't sleep around, and when they try me in a way out of God, I let them know quickly that I'm not the one for that; that my salvation means more to me than that five minutes with them and hell running over with such types in it. This is food for thought. What has the greater reward, heaven, or hell? You choose which one means more to you. Five minutes with them or enteral burning in hell behind them? Well, I know that's not a rational choice for me, ever!

The mercy and grace of God have made me wiser than that. I know people that serve in the church every week and have been in the same church for more than twenty years. They have had babies out of wedlock and still sleep around, and they have never had any growth within their lives. Now they try to tell me how to live, but they aren't living by anything themselves, and my statement to them is, I'm good right where I'm at! Leadership is, by example, and their example is not for me. For if you don't know where you're standing in Christ, then you're honestly not in a relationship with Him because He guides you in everything in your life. You must trust in Him at all times and not on other people around you. They aren't looking out for your soul salvation because they aren't taking care of their soul, I believe that. They are happy right where they are, and they don't ever see any wrong in them, but they sure can find some mistakes in you. It takes a true Christian to have will power over the enemy at all times within their lives.

People are more than eager to follow people with what looks good, but which is not good for them. When they truly don't have real guidance within their lives, they will follow anybody to nowhere because they are too trustworthy of people. I've found times that I've let people put things in my spirit that weren't good for me. I quickly snap out of it. I realize who and who's not there for my own good. Then I let them keep playing the game because it's all on them but not on me, but I don't tell them any different, then I win.

If they think that they got you, they are rejoicing in their own sin ties in their lives and not in yours, and the power of God is still keeping you strong after the storm. I always like to tell people that you can learn a lot from a dummy if nothing else, then how to not be one. Some people get it, and some never do because they keep trying the same thing and never grow because they are getting the same results. They never move forward but stay stuck stupid all their life, and that's not what God wants for us, but we never try to do better for ourselves and still sit in the church. Have you ever seen the ones sitting in church, and everybody knows you better not say anything to them. They don't clap and hug, and they aren't doing anything with others in the church, but still sitting there holding down the spot on that pew where they have been sitting 30 years long without any shift change within their lives of any kind, and they say they are going to heaven with you.

Well, I don't have a heaven or hell to put anyone in, but for the Holy love of God, I just can't understand where the spirit of God is in them, and why all those years they have never truly committed their selves to Him. They have never seen that they had no growth in Christ, and the preacher was preaching, but they weren't listening to him or receiving anything from him, and that's sad.

Conclusion

This concludes the first part of my second volume of God's Grace. I will follow it up with God's Mercy and continue telling my account of daily life. I hope that you all can understand the message of God and put Jesus' teaching in your life to grow into a better person.

A LITTLE DOSE OF GRACE OF JESUS

CECE

www.ingramcontent.com/pod-product-compliance
Lightning Source LLC
Chambersburg PA
CBHW021148090426
42740CB00008B/1002